PRAISE FOR COR

ELFLING: 1st prize, Teen
I AM MARGARET & *BANE'S EYES.* finalists, *CALA Award 2016/2018.*
LIBERATION & *THE SIEGE OF REGINALD HILL:* 3rd place, *CPA Book Awards 2016/2019.*

Corinna Turner was awarded the **St. Katherine Drexel Award** in **2022.**

PRAISE FOR *ELFLING*

I was instantly drawn in

EOIN COLFER, author of *Artemis Fowl* and former Children's Laureate of Ireland.

PRAISE FOR *DRIVE!*

A cross between Jurassic World *and* Mad Max!
Fun, fast paced. And sets up an incredible new world.
I read it three times in two days!

STEVEN R. MCEVOY, blogger at BookReviewsAndMore

PRAISE FOR *WILD LIFE*

How I wish these books had been written when I was a child! Highly recommended action and adventure for dino enthusiasts of all ages!

KATY HUTH JONES, author of *Treachery and Truth*

Darryl and Harry may be safe for now, but they still have a lot to learn from the hunter Joshua about living in the wild. The stakes are rising in this unmissable new entry in the unSPARKed series, an adventurous tale of family drama, faith, and dinosaurs!

DR. LISA THEUS

A couple of teenagers trying to put their family back together... while learning how to hunt dinosaurs, and making sure that they don't end up being hunted themselves. An entertaining premise, compelling— and admirable—young characters, and skillful fast-paced writing. Hard to put down.

MARIE C. KEISER, author of *Heaven's Hunter*

ALSO BY CORINNA TURNER:

† **Coming Soon**
* **Awarded the Catholic Writers Guild** *Seal of Approval*

5

CORINNA TURNER

unSeen

WILD LIFE

CORINNA TURNER

DARRYL

The habitat vehicle's wheels slip slightly as we crest one final rise, but we come safely into the small rocky dell. Halfway up the main valley side, it lies bathed in early morning light and deep shadow. Joshua brings the HabVi to a halt, flicking switches and running through his parking sequence—handbrake, closing the shutters, etc.—without even looking as he peers blearily out the windshield. As soon as he has a hand free he flicks through a few camera views on the dash console and makes a satisfied noise. His arms fold across the steering wheel and his head sinks onto them...

He starts to snore softly.

"Uh, Josh? Don't you want to go to bed properly?" I ask.

No response. Well, no wonder he's beat. He's been driving all night, despite his infected foot and the

1

antibiotics he's taking for it. Harry's been asleep on my shoulder for the last two hours, leaving it to me, as his responsible big sis, to try and keep Josh awake. This dell—this whole valley—is a quiet, out of the way, safe place, so Josh has been telling me for hours. He was determined to reach it before stopping. And, thank God, we're finally here.

"Harry, wake up." I shake my brother's shoulder until he snorts and sits up.

"Urrh-we-there-yet?" he blurts sleepily.

"Yep. Help me get Josh to bed, then we can turn in."

Harry stumbles upright and gets out of the way while I locate Josh's sleeping bag stuffed in a nook near the ceiling, lay it out, and unzip it. Fortunately, since Josh is eighteen and much bigger than sixteen-year-old me or thirteen-year-old Harry, when we both start pulling on him, he wakes up enough to stumble a few steps across cab and flop onto the seat-bed. I ease his boots off—he flinches and murmurs something unintelligible as I do his injured foot—but soon we've got him in his sleeping bag and the bag zipped halfway up and we're tip-toeing through into the living area. Though I suspect we could make as much noise as a triceratops in a china shop and he wouldn't wake up.

"Do we need to, like, check for danger or anything?" asks Harry, blinking and yawning.

"I dunno. I doubt Josh would just go to sleep if we did. Look, you go through the shower and get to bed.

I'll pop up the turret until you're done, just in case."

Our brief overnight stay in the HabVi last night already impressed upon us the importance of daily showers to remove tasty mammal scent, so that's one thing I'm sure we are supposed to do, now it's going to be our home for a while.

Wearily, I climb up the ladder to the turret and open the shutters, looking around to get my bearings. At the other end of the dell the slope comes up at an angle a vehicle can climb—a HabVi, anyway, as we just proved—but, here, we're parked at a safe distance from where the grass drops off into a cliff. Lush spring grass covers the floor of the dell, but the walls are bleak crags, devoid of vegetation, collapsed at one end.

I sit and scan those surrounding crags for predators or threats, but the only things that move are rabbits, quickly creeping back out to nibble grass on the other side of the dell. There's nothing else to be seen, and nothing shows up on the infrared cameras. I guess Josh already checked this.

Unfastening my braid, I comb out my shoulder-length brown hair with my fingers while watching some more. When Harry calls up that he's done, I'm all too happy to shower and crawl up into the 'master bedroom' over the cab. My quadravian Kiko flutters in after me, making soft confused sounds as he settles to roost on my rifle the moment I place it on the wall rack, drawing his four wing-limbs up around him.

3

"Yeah, I know it's morning, we're all out of sync. Sorry, Kiko," I murmur, sliding into my sleeping bag. I've said about fifty chaplets back and forth with Josh as we tried to keep each other awake, but a specific one in thanks for our escape from that awful social worker and for our safe arrival would be nice. Yeah, I...I should...

I wake up with the memory of our predicament still in the forefront of my mind, so maybe I didn't sleep that deep. But when I touch the screen beside the door at the foot end of the berth, the time is almost five in the afternoon. Since I put clean clothes on after my shower, I simply slip back into my jacket—oh boy, the pyx is in there again, what am I going to do with it?—re-braid my hair, then quietly climb down into the living area, followed by Kiko. Deep silence grips the vehicle— Harry and Josh must still be sound asleep.

The triceratops calf in the vehicle's small rear pen gives a low, mournful call as I make a cup of instant coffee with hot water from the boiler tap, but I can't do more than murmur softly to her. Josh was very clear about Harry and me not going in with her until she's tamer. Carefully, I climb the ladder to the turret, one-handed. Leaving the hatch open so I can see if one of them gets up, I open the shutters and settle down with my coffee to enjoy the novelty of a country view. That is, a wild, unfamiliar country view.

We're out in some of the most remote country we

4

could have driven to in one night, right in the middle of nowhere. Josh knew exactly where to go. Maybe this is where he hid after his uncle died and he was waiting to turn eighteen. When he was afraid social workers might take his HabVi and make him stay in-city. Just like they were about to take Harry and me from our farm and force us in-city, regardless of what we wanted.

I frown, my enjoyment of the quiet scene marred. What are we going to do? It's not just that we don't *want* to live in-city. There's also Dad. Josh is sure he was kidnapped, not eaten by a raptor, and that means he may still be alive, and someone will eventually ask for ransom. But no one does hostage swaps in cities, rat traps that they are, surrounded by their huge electric fences with only a few ways in or out. If we go in there, the people who have him—rogue hunters, most likely—will simply kill him and dispose of the evidence. We *have* to stay free. Yet if we're roaming the wilds avoiding anywhere social workers might lurk—how will the kidnappers contact us?

Kiko flutters to the window and peers out, but makes no move to go outside. He still bears the cut from a raptor fang that he acquired the day before yesterday despite me tossing him out of our bogged-down truck to give him a chance of survival. No surprise he's jumpy. I feel that way myself. First Dad gets snatched by a raptor—except it was just meant to *look* that way. Then our new step-mom Carol's too nervous to stay on

5

the farm alone and tries to drive us back to the city. Panics and crashes the truck. Josh arrives in the nick of time, saving Harry and me from the raptor pack, but not poor terrified Carol, who's too scared to move. We get home and try to settle down, with Josh to help with the farm work, and that awful Fernanda woman promptly turns up and tries to take us away. It's been a heck of a two days.

Two days. Has it really only been two days?

A soft noise from downstairs and I glimpse Josh treading across the living area, a bundle of clean clothes under his arm. Clearly intent on catching up on his missed shower, so I don't call down to him. Quiet noises from below for a while, including some happy gulping sounds from the calf. Then he climbs up the ladder, damp-haired, holding his own mug of coffee, settling into another swivel seat with a sleepy smile.

"I put—" he pauses to yawn jaw-crackingly, then continues, "I chucked a hunk of freeze-dried Edmo meat and some potatoes in the food processor. It'll hydrate and cook it all fast enough. I'm guessing we're all ready for a meal."

"Absolutely." The only reason I didn't look for some breakfast was because I thought everyone would want a proper meal as soon as they woke up. "Is the calf okay? I wondered if I should feed her, but you did say..." I shrug.

Josh nods approvingly. "I did, so you were right to

stick to it. And yeah, she's fine. She'd had that many feeds the last twenty-four hours, she was only just starting to get really hungry. No harm done."

"Good. Josh…" I feel cruel asking this before he's even sipped his coffee, but I can't help it, "what are we going to do now?"

It all seemed so clear last night, that we simply *must not* let ourselves be taken to the city, for Dad's sake even more than our own. But this morning, things look a little *less* simple. I mean, we weren't *wrong*, but…

Josh shrugs. "Well, we'd better lie low for a week or two, give that Fernanda baby-snatcher time to move on to other things. Then we can try and meet up with another 'Vi—people I trust—and find out if it's safe to go in-city. If it's not we'll have to get other hunters to put their ears to the ground for us in the 'Vi park, listen out for rumors about your dad. And…have you got a messaging account?"

"Yeah. Don't use it much."

"Good. First thing of all, we need to get your account number out on the grapevine, so the kidnappers know they can get word to you and it's worth keeping your dad. Although—" He breaks off, grimacing.

"Although what?"

"Well," he speaks reluctantly, but honestly, stroking Kiko as he seeks attention. "If they find out that you're with me, they'll know they're dealing with other

7

hunters, not just farm folk—and that could put them off, big time."

With reason, from what I know about hunters and their readiness to administer their own justice. Josh certainly hasn't given any indication he thinks we should pay ransom. Find out where Dad is and "go and get him," that seems to be Josh's plan and if any kidnappers get in the way I suspect he's happy for them to make their excuses to the Almighty.

"Is there…is there any chance at all they'd just…let him go?"

Josh's eyes fill with pity. "Why would they risk it? They don't even have to kill him themselves if they're squeamish—which they're probably not if they've started on this in the first place. Just tie him up, cut him a bit, toss him out of the 'Vi and drive off. No body, no evidence, they're in the clear."

I swallow hard, imagining the carni'saurs gathering around Dad, bleeding and helpless on the ground…

"Aw, sorry." Josh frowns. "I didn't need to go into that much detail, I guess…"

"It's fine, Josh. I won't faint."

I kinda feel ready to puke, but I won't mention *that*. Especially since… "If they're going to be afraid to come near other hunters to do the deal…is there even any hope, still?"

Josh grimaces again. "Hope of getting him back alive, yes, still some. Hope of managing it without

8

paying ransom and with the kidnappers getting their just desserts, very little. That baby-snatcher has put an end to any chance of that."

"So you think we could still get him back if we pay a ransom? But not any other way?"

"Yeah. Once the kidnappers know about me—which they likely will, now you're here in the 'Vi—then they're gonna be super-wary. No way we'll just be able to round up a few friends once we find who has him, waltz in and snatch your dad back. But they might still be willing to set up a super-cautious exchange. It's not good, though. Everyone will be on edge, itchy trigger fingers, super-dangerous."

"Hang on..." My stomach, briefly steadied by his words, goes into freefall again. "Ransom...that means lots of money, right? How are we going to even get it? I won't have access to Dad's accounts until I'm eighteen. And if they think we can't get money"—panic rises again—"they'll kill him!"

"Calm down. That's the second thing we need to take care of. That neighbor of yours, the rich one, your not-actually-guardian—Maurice Carr? Think he'd be good for a loan?"

"For this? Definitely!"

"Okay, then. That's what we need to spread around. Your messaging number and that your neighbor is good for the money."

"Spread it around? I thought it was important to

9

keep it quiet so the police didn't get involved."

"Spreading it among hunters ain't likely to get back to the cops. And we don't have any choice, now. They've gotta know you can get the money or it's over. Anyway, I'm not suggesting we make it explicit. Just spread the two facts, as facts. Darryl and Harry Franklyn can be contacted at this messaging account, and they have a close neighbor who's flush with cash. Okay, a lot of hunters are gonna figure out roughly what that's probably about, but never mind. They're all the more likely to oblige and pass it on to every other hunter they meet if they realize it's important."

I groan and put my face in my hands. That Fernanda woman has complicated everything so badly. Has she as good as killed Dad?

"There's still hope, Darryl." Josh speaks firmly. "I'll send a message to our closest friends, get them to head in-city, start spreading those facts, and see what the situation is. Then we can meet up with them in, say, a week or so, once they've got something to tell us. And we'll take it from there. In the meantime, I'll start getting you two trained up so we're ready to take some contracts when things quiet down. 'Cos there's no telling how long it'll be before things happen with your dad."

Or if they ever will? I push that thought aside and raise an eyebrow. "Train us up? We're pretty good shots already."

Josh laughs so hard he almost spills the last of his coffee. "Oh, so you think all there is to hunting is being a good shot, do you?"

Huh. My cheeks go hot. "Yeah, okay, I guess there is more to it. But we've hunted raptors often enough."

Josh chortles harder and my face gets hotter still. Yep, I'm digging myself in deeper, aren't I? "Fine, I guess we do need training."

He grins and drains his cup without saying any more. Then his eyes flick to the side and focus on something behind me, out in the valley.

HARRY

Thud. Thud. Thud. I jerk awake to the sound of someone stamping on the floor above me.

"Harry?" Darryl's voice. "Get up here, quick!"

"Huh?" I lurch upright, my head colliding with the low ceiling of the cramped cupboard bunk, then grab my rifle and slide the door open. "What's wrong?" I yell.

"Oh, nothing wrong. But get up here; you'll want to see this."

Well, *that's* helpful. I scramble down quickly into the living area, using the footholds this morning, and scoot up the ladder into the turret.

"What?" If it comes out grumpy, well, she's sitting there with her coffee mug, and there's Josh with his,

11

and they've clearly both woken up in their own time and chosen to get up, unlike me with my bruised head...

"*Look!*" Darryl gestures behind me, through the window.

I turn—and gasp. A longneck's huge head is right on a level with us. Clearly the cliff is the height of a longneck. Glancing behind it, I can see others, filling the valley, some, like this one, up on the valley sides, closer to our altitude. I soon look back at the one that's on a level with us. I've never been this close to one. Not to its *head*, anyway.

"Wow."

"Yep." Darryl sounds smug. Yeah, okay, so I'm glad she woke me.

"This is a good place to see them," remarks Josh. When I glance at him, he's looking at the longneck with pleasure, but none of our breathless awe. "The valley is one of the few routes they can take through these mountains, so they often pass through."

We sit and watch the herd. The really close mare moves onwards, but soon a bull comes alongside the cliff, his head towering right over us. In herbi'saurs, the male is usually larger, a reversal of the norm with carni'saurs. Its incurious gaze sweeps over the dell, finding nothing of interest, and the huge creature plods on its way, bringing up the rear.

"Phew." I shake my head as I look after it. Even the proportionally tiny head is large, close up. "I always

12

forget just how big they are."

"Massive," says Darryl.

"Yep," Josh agrees. "So, first lesson. Why did I park here?"

"Up here in the dell?" asks Darryl. "Or the precise place you parked up here?"

"We'll get to the second. But starting with the dell."

I glance down at the longnecks, at the trail of broken foliage and overturned bushes they've left in their wake. Even some quite large boulders have been turned over by their feet in passing.

"I guess...you don't want one of those to knock us over and step on us?"

"Good, Harry. So, how did I know it was a danger?"

"Local knowledge?" suggests Darryl.

"Yes, that's part of it. You're always safer in an area you know, that's something to be aware of. But most threats you can anticipate, if you have enough experience. So, how would you have known this was a comparatively narrow space through which herds of longnecks not uncommonly travel?"

Darryl's eyes move over the valley bottom, hunting for clues. "I don't know...just, local geography?"

Josh nods. "That plays a part, yes." He taps at the console for a moment, bringing up a map. "See here, open land with large forested areas, good for longneck herds. And here, on the other side of these mountains, two big wooded valleys. Also very desirable grazing for this type of 'saur. And see the contours of the various passes—uh, you both know how to read map contours, right?"

"Of course!" That comes out rather indignantly. Dad taught us both to map-read. *Dad...* for a moment my insides knot up. Is he alive? Darryl just nods.

"Good, that puts you ahead of any of my previous assistants," says Josh. "Well, it's pretty clear from the contours that this is the only fairly low-lying, flattish pass large enough to allow longnecks to pass from the forested valleys to the open areas. Making it likely—though not certain—that they might frequent it. That would be enough to make me check for other signs. Any idea what they might be?"

Lesson, he said, and there's something very teacher-ish about his manner. Darryl seems so attentive and eager to perform well, and he just compared us with his last assistants—I guess we are his students. Trainee hunters! What would Fred say if he knew?

"Boulders," Darryl says. "They look like they get turned over quite often. Even the big ones."

Josh grins. "Very good. One of the best signs of longneck herds on the move, that is. And toppled trees in forested areas. What else?"

"Well...if we were close enough, we might see old tracks or dung?"

"Yep, if you go down there, you'll find plenty of

14

both. Anything else?"

Darryl hesitates. "Um…I'm running out of suggestions, though I'm guessing you'd find a hundred little things down there that would tell *you* they'd been here often."

Josh nods. "You're right; there are loads of tiny signs. For example—this is a neat one—you'll even find dents in riverbanks from their chins, when they put their heads right down to scoop the smooth pebbles from the streambed. They swallow them, to help grind up the food in their stomach—though I guess you two probably know that."

Darryl's turn to nod. "Yeah, some of our 'saurs do the same."

"And then there's—" Josh breaks off as my stomach lets out a massive rumble, then grins. "Yeah, I know how you feel. That food should be about done. Let's go down and eat."

"Can we finish off getting the meal ready while you send that message?" asks Darryl, following Josh down the ladder.

What message?

"Yeah, good idea. I'll get it done."

By the time I've climbed down, Josh is seated at the main console, calling up what looks like a standard Net messaging program.

"What message?" I ask Darryl, just as Josh says, "What's that account, Darryl?"

Darryl reels off her own messaging account number, before glancing at me. "Josh is getting our contact details out among hunters so—Lord willing—the kidnappers will end up with them and know they can still get in touch with us. And that Uncle Mau is good for the ransom. It's important they know that, too, as soon as possible."

I swallow as I process this. Okay, this whole getting-Dad-back thing hasn't got any simpler, has it, thanks to the social worker? "So we're paying ransom, then? I thought we were just going to rescue him."

Darryl makes a face. "No choice, now. They'll be wary once they know we're with Josh."

I don't blame them. Josh seems ever so nice and really generous and everything, but heck, is he tough. And he's probably got a bunch of friends equally tough. And maybe not quite so nice. I wouldn't want them after *me*.

"But they'll still want to trade?"

"Hopefully."

I frown as Darryl starts opening kitchen cupboards and figuring out what she needs. Everything about rescuing Dad is so uncertain. I mean, assuming he's still alive, even now...

"There's no point moping, Harry." Darryl must have seen my expression. "Can you unfold the table?"

No point moping. I guess she's right about that.

JOSHUA

I press the auto-send button and simply slide my seat over to the table, since Darryl's just placed the last plate onto it. "Okay, that will go as soon as a satellite gets in range. Technicolor will head in-city as soon as they pick it up—well, barring them having anything really urgent to do—and find out what's what. And start spreading that info around." When they look slightly confused I add, "Technicolor is a 'Vi."

Their faces clear, and they make noises of understanding.

"Do you trust them?" asks Darryl.

"Oh, yeah. They're our—y'know, the Wilson 'Vi's—best friends ever since we came to Exception State. I guess I should just say *my*, now." I glance at the photo frame. My insides have been feeling pretty tight since I got up to the turret this morning and looked out at the dell, but they contract even more at the sight of Dad and Uncle Z there on the wall with their arms around my ten-year-old self. I try to push the feeling away, speaking briskly. "Yep, we've often done team-ups with them. I'd trust them with my life—or your dad's."

"So you told them we're with you?"

"Nope. They'll guess, considering what I asked them to do, but this way if anyone asks they can honestly say they know nothing."

"Ah." Darryl nods and smiles approvingly. Harry, busy scooping meat and potatoes onto a plate, just

17

grunts slightly.

Yeah, I'm certainly ready for this meal. I'm still tired after the all-night drive. And that makes it harder to ignore how painful it is being here. Mebbe I should've gone somewhere else. Nah. This is a tried and tested hide-out. And I've been wanting to visit, anyway. I'm just tired. Another night's sleep and it'll be fine.

Right, Saint Des?

"Uh, Josh?" My head's nodding over my empty plate when Darryl speaks hesitantly.

"Huh? Yeah?"

She touches an uncertain hand to her jacket. "Uh, you know farms often have their own home tabernacle?" She sees my blank look. "You know, like in a Catholic church? An ornate metal safe where Our Lord is kept under the form of bread?"

A dim recollection of what she's talking about stirs in my mind. "Oh, er...yeah, I know. Kinda." Dad mentioned Holy Bread a time or two, but he seemed a bit short on details himself. He always said when I was older we'd find a priest to instruct me and give me some 'Sacraments,' he called them. And him and Uncle Z, too, 'cos apparently they'd missed at least one. But whenever he began to seriously consider it, he got scared I wasn't old enough yet and the priest would call the social workers and have me taken away. And I got scared too. And I think even Uncle Z was scared. So nothing ever happened.

18

"Well," Darryl says, "I couldn't just leave Our Lord in the tabernacle at home when I didn't know when we'd be back. So I've got the pyx—that's the smaller container that goes inside the tabernacle—right here inside my jacket. But I can't keep carrying it around. Where can I put it safe?"

I scratch my nose, my mind over-revving. Our Lord? Our Lord *under the form of bread?* "Um, 'Our Lord' is, er, God, right?"

Darryl nods.

"So...so...you've got Holy Bread in your jacket that's really God?"

"Uh-huh."

"*Oh boy.*" Dad always did seem to think that Holy Bread was very important. I guess this is why. "Um..." I stare around the 'Vi. "So, uh, we need somewhere that's really safe...but...like, honorable?"

"Yeah, ideally."

"Okay, uh...well, you could put It...er...Him...in a cupboard up in the master bedroom. Or...the glovebox in the cab is where we keep important documents, birth certificates and things. That's *kinda* a bit honorable, I guess, but very little room. Or...the gun cabinet. That's the most secure place. There's a little explosives box at the top that's not got much in. I can't actually empty it, because that stuff's gotta be isolated real good, but there'd be space. We could, uh, drape the explosives with some cloth to make a special place."

19

Darryl glances at Harry, but he just shrugs. She sighs. "Um...yeah, maybe the last one. Gun cabinet. The other two just seem too...casual. And not as secure."

"Okay. Let's, uh, get this figured out." Most of my stuff is still in the drawers and cupboards up in the master bedroom—I need to do something about that now it's Darryl's berth. But for now I just climb up and hunt for something fit for God. But I just don't have anything elaborate that would fit. After much fruitless rummaging around for what I know don't exist, my hand touches something wrapped in a carefully folded plastic bag. Part of me wants to just move on and pretend it's no use, but...

Reluctantly, I pull the package out and let the contents slide into my hands. An old shirt of Dad's, the one I simply put away and haven't worn. When I raise it to my face, a hint of Dad still tickles my nose. My throat swells and I have to just sit for a moment, clutching the shirt tight and fighting to breathe. If I use this it will simply smell of C4 and dynamite soon enough. But Dad's scent won't last much longer, anyway... And... And...

Eventually I get hold of myself and climb back down.

"I just don't have *anything* fancy," I tell Darryl, "but this...I guess this is the most precious thing I've got. It was...it was my dad's." The last few words come out squeakier than I intended. Yep, I definitely need some more sleep.

Darryl's eyes widen slightly. "Are you...are you sure you want to use it for this?"

"Yeah. I can't offer quality, but I can offer...this." I hold out the shirt.

Darryl doesn't take it. "Well, *you* should set up the tabernacle. It's your 'Vi."

"Oh. Okay."

I unlock the gun cabinet, and then the inner explosives box. The contents are all present and correct, just a few basics for use with rock or tree falls. Or not for use at all, if things go right, hence they're slightly dusty, despite their sealed environment. The memory of when I last used any tightens my throat again. I double-check the burner is switched off before pulling them out and cleaning them off. Then I re-stack them at the back, adjusting the bracing bars to hold them in place, and arrange Dad's shirt over them. A perfect flat cloth for the thing to stand on it's not going to be, no chance, so I make it into a little nest instead, arranging more bracing bars ready to secure it. Or It. Or Him?

"There. Is that okay?"

Darryl peeps in. "Perfect!"

"Hey, I guess we can have Adoration, then," says Harry. "You wouldn't even need to take the pyx out of there."

"Yeah. That'll be nice."

Adoration? They were talking about that yesterday

21

evening and I was going to ask about it when the baby-snatcher showed up. But Darryl's just taken something about the size of my palm, wrapped in oilcloth, from her jacket, and Harry's gone down on his knees on the metal floor. God...right. I drop down beside him, though my injured foot protests at being bent like that. *Shut up, foot. It's God.*

Darryl takes the oilcloth off, revealing the foot of a little metal case protruding from under a lacy white veil. Leaving the veil on, she reaches up and carefully places the case—the pyx?—in the center of the little nest and tightens the bracing bars. Then she kneels down too and she and Harry recite a prayer and then sing a simple, repetitive song. By the third time through, I can join in too.

O Sacrament most Holy, O Sacrament Divine, it goes. *All praise and all thanksgiving, be every moment thine.* This must be one of the Sacraments Dad talked about.

Then Darryl and Harry bow and Darryl rises to close the explosives-tabernacle. I get up to lock it, finding a place to tuck the oilcloth case in the gun cabinet before closing that. But I immediately open it again.

"Oh yeah, you two, come here. I need to enter your handprints so you can open this if you need to. See, there's the rex gun, there's the scatter gun for piranha'saurs. In an emergency, don't hesitate to grab either. Well, in an emergency you can use anything in

22

here, but you know what I mean. Okay, hand, Harry..."

But as I deal with these practical matters, part of me keeps thinking about that little metal case. I've got *God* in my gun cabinet. Like, *actually*.

That's one Stowaway I didn't anticipate.

DARRYL

When I get up in the morning I glimpse Josh up in the turret already. The triceratops calf shuffles around in her pen a bit, but there's nothing but silence from Harry's bunk. The scent of oatmeal fills the air, and sure enough, there's some waiting in the omni-processor. Based on the empty bowl on the table Josh ate his downstairs, but I balance my bowlful on top of a mug of coffee to carry it up the ladder, my rifle slung over my shoulder.

"Morning," he says.

"Morning, Josh." I sit and look out eagerly to see what there is to see. I never thought before about how much wildlife you see from a 'Vi. There's only a few rabbits nibbling, though. Nothing to see out in the valley.

By the time we finished setting up the tabernacle and programming the gun cabinet, we didn't do a whole lot else, yesterday. Josh ran through some very basic safety procedures, mostly concerning odor control and codewords for concisely warning of danger—not all of which I've got memorized yet—and he finished it up with a run-down of what he called "Vi rules'—which are apparently designed to enable hunters to live together for months in a small metal box without killing each other. *Someone wants space, give them space,* seems to be the first and foremost. The Wilson 'Vi also has a no alcohol rule, not that that affects Harry or me. Although not all HabVis do, apparently it's quite common and viewed as sensible on a number of levels. What some guys do back at their camps being another matter, as Josh said dryly.

Then since we were all yawning and drooping every which-way, we ate a light meal and went to bed. Josh looks brighter this morning, though.

"How's your foot?" I ask.

"A *lot* better. Really healing up, now."

"Well, that's good." Doubly good, now we've had to run off like this. Last thing we need is him getting really sick. Practically everything he says brings home just how much we have to learn. No wonder he was laughing at me.

I eat hungrily, so busy looking around for wildlife in between bites of oatmeal and sips of coffee that it takes me a while to realize that Josh has the drone up, alternating between looking at the view from its cameras on the screens and looking out of the windows.

"Is there anything interesting out there?" I ask eventually, sipping the last of my coffee. I guess that's one way to find wildlife.

He shakes his head. "Nah. Happily. I'd like to go outside for a bit. Could you provide cover?"

"Uh...yeah, of course." His casual question takes me aback. "But shouldn't we wait for Harry to be up too?"

He shakes his head again. "Nah, not necessary. I've been monitoring for an hour. Big carni'saurs almost never come up this high, anyway—no prey large enough for them. This is the far western end of a pair of deinonychuses' territory, but no sign of them this morning. And there's a local pack of velociraptors but with the 'Vi so close I'm not worried about *them*. Ain't seen them either, anyway. And that's it. It's a very safe location. You and your rifle will be more than enough."

"Well, okay then. You're the boss." Literally.

All the same, when, with no more ado, he slips his ear piece in, climbs quickly down the ladder and lets himself out the side door, it feels like a crushing weight of responsibility has landed on my shoulders. Silly, because I've provided solo cover for Dad or Harry routinely in the outer pastures at home. But the chances of a predator venturing there are low, whereas here, totally unSPARKed, outside any electric fence...

I mean, Josh hasn't even taken his rifle along. Though that might be deliberate. At one point yesterday he mentioned something about it often being better not to take a rifle outside unless you were planning to use it because of the risk of getting tempted to make some stupid stand instead of getting safely back in the 'Vi.

To my relief he simply walks across to where the crags have collapsed, spilling soil, loose stones, and larger rocks onto the far side of the dell, and stops there, placing his palm flat against the largest boulder. After a moment, he kneels quietly in front of it, his head bowed.

Looking through the sights of my rifle, it's only then that I make out writing carved into the rock. Crude text, clearly not the work of a master stonemason, but cut firm and deep. Two names: 'Isaiah Wilson' and 'Zechariah Wilson.' There are two sets of dates, too, but they're smaller and I can't read them very well. The last dates seem to be less than two years apart, though. Heck, poor Josh. To lose both his dad and his uncle in such a short time. And growing up with just them, alone out here in a 'Vi—they must've been his entire world.

No wonder, despite his obvious love for his way of life, he seems a bit melancholy at times. "I've had five assistants in the 'Vi since I turned eighteen," he told me, when I asked, "city-folk, all of them, plus one velociraptor and, honestly? I got on best with the raptor!" Well, I think he likes Harry and me better than a raptor, so hopefully our parental losses are his gain.

Uh oh, I mustn't let something creep up and eat him while I'm sitting here feeling sorry for him. Quickly, I focus my attention on the screen, grabbing the drone's joystick to do a quick circuit of the area and familiarize myself with the landscape. No sign of danger, though. Some small herbi'saurs graze higher up the mountain and a large bird of prey sits on an outcrop, preening, but hardly anything else moves in the morning stillness.

JOSHUA

The boulder is cool and rough under my fingertips as I trace the writing absent-mindedly. My fingers were bleeding by the time I'd finished the carving, though I was in no state to care. The scent brought the velociraptors and the deinons down on me, quick enough, which forced me to pull myself together.

I put Dad's name first, because this is where we held his hair burial—an accumulation of hair clippings wrapped in another of his shirts as a...a substitute. But the wooden cross Uncle Z and I set up at the time got swallowed by the rockfall, after I collapsed the cliff to bury Uncle Z. That traditional six feet deep ain't enough to keep big carni'saurs from digging a fella up. You gotta go very, very deep or get creative. I just laid Uncle Z in a shallow grave and stuffed some dynamite into the cracks where the cliff was almost ready to come down anyway. Ain't no carni'saurs getting to him now.

I lean my forehead against the cold stone, the memory of Dad's scent from the shirt filling my mind, filling me in turn with a memory of him holding me

27

tight in his arms. Of Uncle Z's arm around me. But it's just memories, now. Now I'm the oldest, the one who's supposed to keep everyone safe. Everything feels flipped around. At least, after all these months of feeling by myself even when I had company, I don't feel so...alone. I'm real glad to have Darryl and Harry for my assistants. They already feel almost like...family.

Thanks, Saint Des. Thanks, God in the gun cabinet.

I just don't want anything to happen to *them*. I need to train them up, real good.

DARRYL

Josh's quiet moment by the grave has gone on some time when I finally catch a flash of movement on the drone cam. A smudge of grey moves, barely visible against the boulders, save for a flash of red. I flick to infrared, checking the silhouette. Could be a raptor, could be an upright herbivore, though from the colors, I'm guessing... I zoom the camera in closer to make sure.

Yep. Velociraptor.

"There's a velociraptor approaching, Josh. In fact..." I check the non-zoomed-in drone cameras on thermal setting. "Yep, the whole pack is on the way."

"Okay, I'll come back in." Josh rises calmly, pausing to touch the marker stone once more before moving towards the 'Vi at a painfully casual pace.

28

"Uh, Josh? They're coming fast."

"Relax, I'm nearly there. Don't shoot them."

As he reaches the 'Vi the first velociraptor appears on the rocks at the edge of the dell, a large female, the size of a wolf, peering towards Josh, her featherless face framed by a reddish-brown ruff. Josh opens the door, swings up into the doorway, then pauses to look back at her. "Oh, hello, Rusty," he murmurs, and only then steps inside and hits the door 'close' button.

I swallow my heart back down into my chest as he climbs up into the turret, but something must show on my face because he gives an apologetic shrug.

"Sorry, I shoulda said. They got real used to me being around, before. Sure, they'd hunt me before long if I stayed out there, but the smell of me don't make them super-aggressive, the way they normally would be."

He settles into a chair, while I lean forward to watch the raptors, now roaming around the 'Vi, sniffing hopefully at the ground. "Are they looking for something?"

"Yeah, scraps," says Josh. "Uncle Z and I were almost due to resupply when he... Well, I couldn't burn fuel driving a distance away every time I needed to dump some offal or food scraps, nor incinerating it, neither. Once I was sure this pack would clear it up before anything larger could scent it, I just...well, used them for waste disposal. It ain't ideal, and I wouldn't do

29

it in a more populated area where it mattered them getting used to people. But this ain't one of those."

"It sure isn't."

The reddish-brown ruffed female, probably the matriarch, takes a run up, bounces off the hood and lands lightly on the roof. She runs right up to the turret, looking in the open window. Her head jerks back suddenly as she sees me, and she darts back a few steps, then turns to cock her head and peer towards us. I sit very still, delighted, now Josh is safe, to see her so up-close. Not so pleased, Kiki flattens himself against my neck, claws digging in as he clings tight. 'Microraptor' may be the scientific name of his species, but quadravians are very different from 'normal' raptors.

My stillness does the trick. She runs closer, her claws tapping the roof, and peeps through the bars again. Josh seems very busy watching the others down in the dell, almost like he's determined to ignore her.

"Now, uh." His shoulders are tense. "I guess you know the law on raptors. No domesticating them, unless you're an army-trainer. Zoo-taming only, ready for sale."

"Yeah, Harry and I both know that. Not that plenty of farmers haven't got busted for keeping a velociraptor in the corner of their barn before now. Usually when they show up at the hospital with serious bite and slash wounds."

"That's the way it goes," says Josh, falling further

into teacher-mode. "'Cos raptors have only three categories for other living things: pack, predator, and prey. If they think you're one of the last two, which they will unless they imprinted on you at birth, then sooner or later they will attack you. So never trust them."

"Is that absolutely true?" I ask, watching the rust-ruffed raptor, still peering in and now making chirping sounds at Josh. Yes, definitely at *him*. "What about Saint Des and his raptor-friend, Beauty? She was never imprinted on him."

Josh shrugs, still determinedly ignoring the matriarch's friendly overtures. "No, she wasn't and, truth be told, I know of a few cases...well, two, including that one, where people have formed a bond with an adult raptor that...that either lasted a long time, or...or held when it really mattered. And yeah, it probably has happened other times, now and then. But those really are the rare exception. Plain suicide to count on it—or even try to bring it about unless you've no other choice."

Bring it about? No other choice? What does he mean by that? Before I can ask, the raptor drops to her haunches, touches one wing claw to the roof, like she's pretending the wing-arm is a weight-bearing limb, and tucks the other wing-arm neatly up to her chest. Eyes still fixed to Josh.

"So, uh, Josh?" I try to sound serious.

"What?" His gaze on the other raptors is taking on a

frantic edge.

"Is sitting up and begging natural velociraptor behavior?"

"Uh..." I can see his brown skin darkening as he flushes. "Uh, no; no it ain't."

"So...just how bored were you, those three months you spent here?"

"Uh," he looks around at last, with a sheepish smile. "Pretty darn bored, yeah. Oh, fine, Rusty. Good girl. You've got a good memory." He pulls a small packet from a drawer, rips it open and tosses something tiny to the raptor, who snatches it from mid-air and swallows it.

"How'd you train her to do that?"

Josh shrugs. "Patience and the right animal. That ain't all she can do. Watch." Giving her his full attention at last, he raises one hand and makes a clear circling motion. Rusty cocks her head, then turns all the way around, finishing with her eyes fixed expectantly on the packet in Josh's hand. He grins and tosses her another training treat. As soon as she's gulped it down, he raises his hand high and makes a little upwards motion. Rusty leaps on the spot, so high it's a reminder why the safe distance from a raptor is always ten times further than you'd think.

"Good girl." He tosses her another treat. "Okay, Rusty, you gonna shake?" He holds out one hand. Rusty approaches the bars again, her eyes darting suspiciously to me. But after a moment she slides a wing-arm through, allowing Josh to take her wing-claw and shake her 'hand' gently.

Josh grins and balances another treat on Rusty's wing-claw. She pokes her head through the bars and brings it to her mouth without dropping it—or snapping at Josh. Kiko trembles against me.

"Heck," I breathe, when she pulls her head out again. "How did you teach her that much in three months?"

Josh shrugs yet again. "Two months. I spent the first month just lying around pretty much wishing I was...well, not doing much, anyway. Then Rusty started to distract me. She's smart and curious and pretty friendly, as wild raptors go. I wouldn't have got that far with most raptors without having them in my 'Vi with me. But I've always been good with critters. Done a lot of zoo-taming, too."

"So, uh, why didn't you just catch her and put her in your pen and zoo-tame her and sell her later on, and then it would've all been legal?"

Another shrug. "Well, I was never *planning* on doing anything with her, was the problem. She's a fine young matriarch, with a mate, in her prime. I would never normally choose her for capture. Unmated young juveniles, or just post-juvenile, with no place in the pack, those are the animals you want for zoos. Uh, Darryl, don't lean back any further."

I glance over my shoulder and recoil forwards into the center of the turret. While we—or at least I—have been distracted by Rusty's performance, two more raptors have gained the rooftop, their muzzles hovering just outside the bars, eyes glinting as though they rather fancy shoulder of farmgirl for breakfast, or perhaps wing-limb of quadravian.

"That's Jill and Jack," Josh adds. "And they ain't very friendly."

Yet another raptor leaps up onto the roof via the hood, but he stays at the far end, calling to Rusty pleadingly. "Oh, and that's Mr. Rusty. I, uh, call him Hinge. Silly, but it makes me chuckle. Quite a nervous boy to have attracted a fine lady like Rusty, truth be told. Though maybe he has hidden depths. Perhaps he's just jealous. He's wary of me, anyway."

Hinge shows no signs of coming closer. When three juveniles leap up as well, clearly feeling left out, he hisses and snaps at them, driving them back to what he clearly considers the greater safety of the grass below.

"What the heck is going on up there?" Harry's voice precedes him through the hatch. "Sounds like a flock of wild turkeys are dancing on the... Oh!"

His eyes fly wide as they fix on the velociraptors, and he goes motionless. With a smooth, inconspicuous motion, Josh slides the pack of treats into his pocket, making Rusty peer and mutter in a disappointed way.

"Shouldn't you, uh, have the windows closed?"

whispers Harry, still staring avidly.

Josh looks amused. "They can't get more than their heads through those bars." But then he shrugs. "Yeah, let's close 'em 'til they go." He pulls a master lever that drops all the windows back into place and busies himself with a console screen, not looking at Rusty.

Maybe it's because the windows are mirrored on the outside and she can no longer see Josh or maybe it's Hinge's plaintive squeaks, but it's not that long before the matriarch leaps down from the 'Vi, the others following her. After one more pass around the vehicle to check for scraps, the pack leaves, Rusty and Hinge at the front again.

Clearly, if Josh has his way, Harry will never know what he missed. And I don't mind. Wouldn't want to give my little brother bad ideas, now would we? Though if we stick around here for long, Rusty will surely give the game away.

HARRY

After testing our aim with some .22s—admittedly at rather short range—by getting us to pop off a few rabbits from the turret, Josh gives us some more lessons. He makes us repeat the important things he told us yesterday and anything we can't he goes over again. Then he adds a load of new stuff. My brain is feeling almost as stuffed and stretched by lunchtime as my stomach is afterwards—after retrieving the rabbits, Josh cooked up some mean rabbit pies while lecturing us.

He's thrown so much info at us, it's a bit of a relief when, once we've finished eating, he announces that we're moving on—surely we'll get a break while we travel?

"So much for this being a neat hide-away where we'd be staying a while," I can't help remarking.

"Sure, it's a quick, safe location to tuck ourselves into in the heat of the moment, as it were," he replies. "No need to think or worry too hard about our destination. But we're rested now and this ain't the best place for training you two up. We'll head further into the wild country for that."

So, by early afternoon, we're driving back down that steep valley side and turning towards the mountains. So much for getting a break while we drive, though. Josh keeps up the flow of info. Darryl listens attentively, asking intelligent questions, and I struggle to do the same, but by the time we pull into another sheltered parking place, also high up, and we've run through 'why did I park here,' my head feels ready to burst.

Darryl suggests we should get our tuteApps out for a few hours—I don't know whether to be furious with her or simply grateful at the thought of a change of subject—but Josh vetoes it.

"It won't hurt you to miss a week of that," he says.

"You can catch up. But this stuff you need to know as soon as possible."

As it begins, so it continues. Okay, other than the constant insistence on us *learning* stuff all the time, it's fantastic. Some stuff is boring or more normal, of course. There's the cleaning. A *lot* of cleaning. *Clean cats, not dirty dogs*, as the hunter saying goes. And it turns out that there's a fold-down set of exercise bars in the main living area, on which Josh usually goes through a vigorous regime of pull-ups and acrobatic maneuvers pre-shower—and clearly assumes we'll do the same, if we have any sense. I guess this is why the majority of hunters look leaner and fitter than you might expect.

But the fantastic stuff is *really* fantastic. Josh thinks nothing of stopping in some wide open area so we can go for a run or by some remote mountain pool so we can swim, always two at a time with one person providing cover.

Though, one day, after a long lesson on monitoring the surrounding landscape for threats, we actually eat a picnic lunch on a high pinnacle of crag, all three of us, the 'Vi in plain sight a short way downslope and the drone hovering above us, heat sensors set, transmitting its thermal and visual feeds to Josh's handPad. As we sit there, the wind in our hair and the wilderness laid out at our feet, the fact that Josh can find places where we can *do* this sort of thing fills me with awe.

But even that turns into a lesson when he starts

showing us different types of lichen and moss, and getting us to memorize their useful properties. This one's edible, this one clots blood, this one makes a mean dye... Worse, they all look *identical*.

By the following day, I can't take any more. My head feels stuffed full and splitting open. Growing mulish from the brain strain, I try to demand an afternoon off, but...

"Two things keep you alive out here, Harry," Josh says sternly, "knowledge and practice. Well, there's only so much I can do to speed up the second, but the first I *can* do something about."

I open my mouth to protest that *yeah, sure, but can't we take it slower*, but he goes on, relentlessly, "This may feel like some fun nature tour to you, Harry, but life out here ain't a game, as you'll find out the first time something goes south."

I can't believe he's saying *no*. He's been hammering us with info for *days*... "Can't we just have a few *hours*...?"

"Did you know," he counters, "that about eighty-three percent of all fatalities happen to young or inexperienced hunters?"

"Yeah?" I snap. "Didn't your *super*-experienced dad get eaten by a rex?"

Oops. I don't need to see Darryl's wince and frown to want to take it back. Too late.

Josh grabs my collar and pushes me back against

the wall. Not slams me into it, just pushes hard enough that I feel his much-superior strength. "Yeah," he says in a very low voice, his face close to mine. "Guess what, my dad got et by a rex *despite* all that experience. Well, you and Darryl are a hundred times more likely to go that way than he ever was, understand? And I'm not anxious to see that happen on my watch. Got *that?* Now wash your ears out and stop whining like a little kid." He releases me and steps away.

Darryl frowns from one of us to the other but doesn't join the argument. I almost shoot her a glare for that, but after Josh's last words I manage not to. Might seem babyish. I've been so happy Josh was treating me like a man, but Dad always did say being an adult was more work than fun. Maybe he was right.

I'm impressed with Josh's self-control, though. If he'd said that about Mom—heck, he could so easily have shot the same thing right back at me about Mom and farming!—I'd've probably tried to punch him. Yeah, I'd rather spend a moment feeling like a little leggy'saur wriggling in an allo's mouth than hear someone get at Mom. I shouldn't have said what I did. Is not reacting much a Josh-thing or a hunter-thing? Although it's hard to imagine such tough guys not playing very rough, Dad always insisted they place a lot of value on restraint.

I clear my throat awkwardly. Manage a just about audible mutter of, "Uh, sorry, Josh."

His familiar shrug, and he says more lightly, "Okay, lunch, then on to survival skills. Things you hope never to need, but when you do, you really do." But he shoots a doubtful look at me, like he's wondering, despite my apology, if the little kid is up to it. Heat rises in my cheeks. If only I'd never said anything...

Darryl finally speaks. "Maybe we should get out our handPads and try taking notes? We're really not used to this amount of oral learning."

"Ain't you?" He runs a hand through his hair and shrugs. "Well, sure. Lunch first."

"Can we picnic again?" I ask eagerly, peering out the window. "What about up there?"

Josh screws his face up in a...yeah, a pained expression. "Harry, picnic sites where the entire 'Vi can go out-vehicle together are very rare. And this one...you think we should picnic there, do you? Well, let's go up the turret and check it out."

I've a sinking feeling as I follow him up the ladder. I've just made a fool of myself again, haven't I?

Yep. Turns out a family of Higher Mountain Bears live just under there. Whoops.

"Getting that close to their den wouldn't be a smart idea," Josh tells us, when he's pointed out the single half-hidden pawmark that was supposed to have tipped me off. "'Saurs ain't the only dangerous things out here, even nowadays."

"Is it true there used to be loads of types of bears?" I

remember that from a history lesson.

"Sure, some zoos even have a few old breeds, still. Big ones, little ones, black ones, even white ones. Most of them were sitting ducks for carni'saurs, though, and died out in the wild. The hybrids survived, like the Higher Mountain Bears. Smaller and faster, hugging the higher slopes where the big carni'saurs don't prowl, digging real deep. Shy and elusive as brown bears, vicious as grizzlies when threatened. They hold their own up here, just about, though wolves often outperform them. Anyway, uh, lunch in the 'Vi today, okay?" says Josh.

I nod, my face on fire.

JOSHUA

"I really ain't trying to be mean, y'know," I tell Darryl the following morning, when, like the fractionally more experienced hunter she's becoming, she climbs up to the turret after eating her oatmeal down below rather than bothering to balance it precariously up the ladder. A lesson she has learned without having to spend fifteen minutes clearing up every last speck of oatmeal from the living area floor, unlike my previous assistants. "I just don't want either of you to get hurt. I'm sorry things got ugly with Harry, yesterday."

Darryl shrugs. "You are working us pretty hard and I know how he feels. But...I also don't want to see him

41

get hurt. So it's hard to feel entirely mad at you."

I shoot her a grin. "Good. I don't want to be the tyrant whose assistants jump 'Vi at the earliest opportunity."

Darryl grins back. "Hardly."

"Good." I take a breath. "Uh, if you don't mind going below again, I've got something to show you. For the, uh, tabernacle." I've been working on it a little each evening, in the privacy of my berth, 'cos I wasn't quite sure what she'd think of it. But it's finished now.

"Oh?" With eager curiosity, Darryl heads quickly back down the ladder, still clutching her coffee. I follow with my empty cup and fetch my handiwork from the cab bedroom.

"Here." I lay it gently on the table. "It's a mat for the, er, pyx to stand on. Feels like it should be stood on something extra."

"You're right." Darryl moves to inspect it. "Usually it stands on a white lace thing"

"Careful handling it," I interrupt, as she reaches for it. "They're not really designed to be moved much."

Her fingers brush the surface of the mat. "Oh, wow, is this feather-lace? Josh, it's beautiful!"

After one touch she takes her fingers away and simply peers at it, admiring the shimmering, multi-colored lacework. "This stuff is supposed to be really hard to make. Takes ages, they say."

I shrug. "True enough. We normally didn't bother

making more than one large piece each in a winter. But this is so small it didn't take so long. And I wouldn't call it *difficult*, exactly. Merely fiddly. A real patience-tester. You just fix the feather ends into a circle, then you work outwards, fastening tufts together with spider-line to make the lace pattern."

"Looks difficult enough to me," Darryl mutters. "But this is great, Josh. It'd be really expensive to buy and it's genuinely beautiful. It's perfect for the tabernacle."

I'm just relieved she likes it. I was a little afraid a feather mat might count as, I dunno, pagan or something, though God made even the raptors that the feathers came from. But it ain't *pagan*, it's a beautiful luxury item. So that's okay.

DARRYL

"But I thought hunter women made all those hunter handicrafts they sell in zoo gift shops and the like," says Harry, after he's exclaimed over the gorgeous feather-lace mat. No one's figured out how to make halfway decent feather-lace by machine yet, which is why the stuff commands a high price tag.

"Sure they do," says Josh. "All year round, in the camps, along with growing the vegetables and raising the kids and all that. But if you ain't got no women in your outfit—and even if you have—you need

43

something to do during those long dark winter evenings. Idle hands earn no keep. We'll collect up some good teeth and claws and feathers and hide throughout the summer and, come fall, I'll be teaching you to make purses and belts and pendants and all."

Harry looks like he's not sure whether to regard this as a promise or a threat. Me, I'd love to be able to make some of those fancy knick-knacks. Still...fall. Will we still be with Josh come fall? Surely we hope to have rescued Dad by then? But if we don't get anywhere with that, then the best we can hope is that we are still with Josh and not in the hands of Fernanda Baby-snatcher, as Josh always refers to her. Josh having a long, fraught history staying one step ahead of the Child Protective Services, who didn't think a child belonged in a Hab'Vi.

We install the mat carefully in the tabernacle that evening, when we have Adoration for the first time. I still haven't had that induction from Father Benedict, but he did say it was okay. I hope the change of location doesn't affect that.

"What *is* Adoration?" Josh asked, when we mentioned it again.

"Uh, it's kind of like...chilling out with God," I said.

"God the Holy Bread?"

"Yeah. But since it's, y'know, *God*, you do it more reverently than you would with a human. But internally you can just chat with God, y'know? Or recite prayers.

44

Or whatever you like."

Josh kneels with us now and stares solemnly at the Host, which I've exposed by turning a little knob to open the spiral lattice in the front of the pyx. He's got a lot of interest and enthusiasm for religious matters, but very little knowledge of anything but Saint Desmond, plain enough. Sounds like his dad tried to pass on everything he knew himself, but the fact Isaiah Wilson ran away from his abusive father at the age of eleven and learned most of what he knew from his mother who died some years earlier still accounts for Josh's ignorance.

Dad and Father Benedict have both emphasized the importance of taking some quiet time like this regularly, however busy you are, and even Harry usually tries to take it seriously, with only occasional grumbles. He doesn't even fidget as much as usual today. Maybe he's thinking about Dad. Or feeling more responsible for himself now that he's being treated like a man. Even Dad didn't quite treat Harry like a man yet. Josh seems willing to accept him on those terms until he proves him wrong—despite yesterday.

I can tell Harry doesn't want to mess up again. He knuckled down a lot more to the learning today. Using the handPads helped. I figured from the beginning Josh is boss and if Josh wants us to work by studying then that's what we should do—quite aside from the obvious safety advantages—and Harry's getting the hang of that now, at the cost of having Josh settle him down like a dominant wolf to an upstart pup.

But Josh has now started peppering his info with hair-raising or outright grisly accounts of what happened to real hunters who got each thing we're learning wrong, and I think despite Harry's sometimes infuriatingly resilient 'sunny optimism,' as he would call it, or 'plain over-confidence' as Dad and I would sometimes have it, the true tales aren't entirely being wasted.

After Adoration we settle down with a bedtime cup of Joe, taking it in turns to give Kiko some attention, but soon a ping sounds from the console.

"Satellite lock," murmurs Josh, abandoning his mug and sliding his chair over to check for messages. Normally it only takes a moment, but this time we can see him opening something and reading it. Finally he swipes it closed and returns to the table. "Okay, we're meeting Technicolor in three days. Sounds like they've got stuff to tell us."

My heart pounds faster, and I can see Harry's eyes widening with hope. "About Dad?" he asks.

Josh frowns. "Doubtful. They don't know anything about that, remember? So, yeah, they could have heard a rumor and put two and two together with what I told them, but it's probably to do with the baby-snatcher. This is good, though. We can hand Trilly over to them, and they can get her to the university."

I guess that way Trilly the Triceratops will end up in her intended home and Technicolor will hand on most of the money to us.

Could they know something about Dad, though? It's going to be a long three days.

HARRY

I thought these three days would crawl by but I'm falling into my bunk each night so tired I'm asleep at once. Josh is increasingly supplementing his oral learning, as Darryl calls it, with practical lessons. He's got us making snares and stripping and reassembling weapons blindfolded—usually with parts from several guns mixed together, just for good measure. Last time he even covered them in slippery mud and timed us. Now we've moved on to stalking. Or, more accurately, hiding. Having covered the basics verbally, we're now working *outside* the 'Vi!

This moment, I'm up in the turret, keeping watch while Josh, having turned his back for ten minutes to give her a chance to hide, now looks for Darryl.

"Can I look too?" I beg. I mean, we've got the heat sensors set and everything...

"Everything still clear?"

"Yep."

"Okay, take a quick look."

I stare out over the flat open area of low

undergrowth and low boulders. No sign of my big sis. I grab the binos and scan the area. "Well, I can't find her." Surely this time she's done it! "So, where is she, then?" I challenge Josh eagerly. She's done it, right? Rabbit pie for dinner! He promised to make more pies the day one of us managed to hide so well he couldn't spot us.

Josh's eyes are still moving over the landscape. After a moment he lifts his own binoculars and focuses.

"Darryl, you're five foot to the right of the boulder at two o'clock. Under the foxglove. Don't eat that, by the way, it's..."

"Poisonous," Darryl and I chorus.

Josh grins. "Good. Makes perfectly good cover, though. Unlike—" He falls silent, biting his lip to tamp down a smile, but I still scowl. Okay, so he *had* shown us itchweed before, along with, like, a trillion other plants. I guess it *was* pretty funny, but at least he doesn't go on about it.

I'm focusing where he just said but I still can't see her, though her groan on my earpiece made it clear he was right. "How the heck do you know she's there?" I demand. "Did you sneak a peep at the thermal scan?"

Josh shoots me a hard look. Oops. Guess I just, er 'impugned his honor' or whatever the saying is. But, the way he usually does when I make a childish gaffe, he ignores it.

"It's an excellent try, Darryl. You're getting good at

this. But you piled slightly too many loose branches over you. There's no reason for a pile to have collected in that shape in that location. And your elbow's sticking out. So, a near miss. But if I can spot you...

"...so can a raptor," we chorus.

He grins. "*Good*," he purrs, like a satisfied cat. Or mountain lion. "Darryl, you good for one more try? Then Harry can have a couple more turns before we call it a day."

My heart sinks. I'm already muddy and prickled all over from half a dozen previous attempts, never mind the itchweed yesterday. But I keep my mouth shut. Dad always said hunting was a hard life so I should've known what I was signing up for, right?

Anyway, Josh says at this rate we can actually take some contracts soon. Then we'll be *real* hunters!

DARRYL

"I thought hunters always hunted from their 'Vis," says Harry, bracing a foot against the dash as the vehicle heaves over a particularly steep ridge. We're en route to meet Technicolor at last! "So," he goes on, "why do you call it 'stalking' not just 'hiding?' It's just for hiding if you end up stuck out-Vi, right?"

"Nope," says Josh, peering ahead as he steers downslope. "You hunt from the 'Vi when you can. But the thing you have to avoid above all is critters

49

associating the 'Vi with danger. Okay, smarter critters like raptors tend to catch on, but you absolutely don't want a situation where herds of large herbi'saurs stampede at the mere sight of a HabVi. That's just super-dangerous for everyone."

He shifts down a gear as we slide slightly on some loose gravel, but carries on speaking, clearly unconcerned. "So, first preference is to cam up the vehicle so they don't associate the hunting with an uncamouflaged 'Vi. Or use natural features to screen the vehicle from them. But if that's no good, someone stays in the 'Vi to provide cover and one or two others circle partly around the herd so the shots come from well away from the vehicle. And then there're those lovely contracts when you have to go into inaccessible terrain on foot to cull something that's really causing problems."

"Raptors?" Harry's eyes go wide.

"Too often, yeah. And I'm telling you, getting to a good position, unseen, and taking them out nice and quick from there is so much preferable to letting them figure out you're trying to sneak up on them. 'Cos then it gets real interesting who's hunting who."

"I bet," I murmur. Heck, will we end up with contracts like that? Was I right to bring Harry into this?

"But we won't be taking none of those any time soon," says Josh firmly, as though reading my mind.

Harry actually looks faintly disappointed. I shake

my head. Josh glances Harry's way, rolls his eyes at me and grins, making me swallow down a laugh. The fact that fearless Josh thinks Harry's a fool to wish for such contracts...says a thing or two about those contracts!

"Oh, ay-up, there they are," Josh says, pointing.

Another 'Vi is moving towards us along the bottom of the valley, large and glinting silver in the sun. My heart starts pounding. *Could* they know anything about Dad?

Josh's hand moves to the headlights and he flashes three times, very deliberately.

"Does that mean something?" I ask.

"Yep. One flash means 'danger.' Two means 'hi and bye.' Three means 'cup of Joe?'"

"And four?" asks Harry.

"By the time you need four, you just get on the interCar and speak to them."

Three flashes come from the headlights of the other vehicle, and soon we're down on the valley floor.

"Is this a safe place to stop?" asks Josh.

Harry and I have been keeping our eyes open so we don't need to peer around much.

"I think so," I say.

"Why?"

"It's wide enough larger herbi'saurs can go around us. And the river's small enough and far enough away from us not to pose a large flood risk."

"Flash floods?"

I lean to check the map, tracing the contours in the surrounding mountains. Harry pushes in, doing the same, so I let him answer.

"Low?"

"Yeah, low," agrees Josh. "Well, as always, that's *obvious* flash flood risk low. You can get them *anywhere*, trust me."

There's something in his voice that suggests personal experience of a negative kind, but we're closing the distance with the other 'Vi fast, now. As we approach, Josh presses the button to retract the wing mirrors. Slowing to a crawl, the two vehicles draw alongside one another, passenger side to passenger side, so close, coming to such a precise halt that…yep, by the time we've stepped through into the living area our side door is sliding back, to reveal the other Vi's door perfectly aligned with it. The gap between the two vehicles is too narrow for anything larger than a very determined piranha'saur to get into.

Three unexpectedly familiar guys step through, each carrying a folding seat. "West? Thiago? Ed?" Harry and I exclaim.

"Hey, kids." West throws us a crooked grin, teeth gleaming in a face much darker than Josh's and with clear African American features.

Hispanic Thiago gives us a tense nod, and fair-skinned, blue-eyed Ed a laid-back smile. All three are somewhat younger than Dad. And…

"Huh, *Technicolor*," says Harry, echoing my thought as his eyes flit between them. "Now it makes sense."

West grins at him, then puts down his seat to give Josh a quick hug and back-slap. "So, Josh, it's true, huh? You have got the kids."

"Well, yeah. Is anyone looking?"

"Is anyone *looking?* Heck, you've stirred up a heap of trouble, boy."

"Police have been crawling over the 'Vi parks," Thiago says, "asking about you. *Has anyone seen you? Does anyone know where you might be?* Some frilly city-lady too, the worst of the lot."

"No one seemed to think it worth asking what Josh were like and whether he'd make a good employer," drawls Ed, holding out an arm for Kiko to land on. "*Well, hello, beautiful.* Heck of a load of fuss about nothing."

"When city-folk get their fuss on, they don't see reason." Thiago speaks tersely. "You know they're right funny about anyone they see as little children. Don't reckon these two are old enough to pick their own employment, is the problem."

"Well, we'll have to stay out-city for a bit until they calm down," says Josh. "You guys will help us out with fuel and contracts, right?"

"They won't just drop it, Josh," says Thiago. "Not the tizzy they were in."

"So we'll stay out as long as necessary. We can, if

53

you help. Will you?"

West puts his hands on his hips and fixes Josh with a measuring look. Thiago scowls.

"Well, mebbe, mebbe not," West says. "What's going on? 'Cos, sorry, I'm not helping you put your head in this noose—let alone putting our heads into it too—just 'cos a couple of farm kids don't want to go in-city awhile. Come on, Josh, they say this girl is eighteen in less'n a year and a half. So she can take guardianship of her kid brother then and go back to her farm and you and us can be in the clear."

"It ain't that simple, West." Josh shoots a questioning look at me and Harry. I raise an eyebrow, questioning back, and Josh nods. He thinks it's safe to tell them. Harry shrugs at me, so I nod to Josh. Sounds like we need their help even more than I realized.

"Look," says Josh, "let's make some Joe and sit down and I'll explain it all, okay?"

"We're listening," says West, unfolding his chair. From the look in his eye, he guesses that there's a lot more to it. No surprise after Josh had him spreading that info around.

Once everyone has a seat and a mug, Josh lays it all out—the faked raptor attack, why we think Dad is more likely kidnapped than murdered, and how Carol's death and Fernanda's interference have thrown everything into jeopardy.

"Huh." West rubs a hand over his stubbly chin

54

when Josh stops talking. "You have found yourself a thornbush, haven't you? I was gonna say—you being such a soft-hearted fella and hating the city so much— that if you really couldn't bear to hand them over to the city-folk you should think of skipping off into another state where they might not be so interested. But that would be about as bad as going in-city, as far as getting their dad back is concerned. I see why you need to stick around. But you sure can't do it without help."

"If you really don't wanna get involved...I'm not trying to get you guys in trouble too," says Josh.

"We're not trying to get *anyone* in trouble," I say, alarmed by how bothered West and the other two seem about helping us. Well, West and Thiago. Ed doesn't seem concerned, but then he seems the horizontally chilled-out type. Right now he's more interested in slipping Kiko treats from his pockets than in dire decision-making.

West snorts. "We're already involved, Josh, because you are. How long do you think those city-folk can keep this up before some snake like Jason Desmoines gives in to the temptation to tell them *something*. And *who your friends are* is rather easier to justify than *where you are*, which would have him in hot water with everyone—not that he knows it to tell, thank Saint Des. Unless you give those kids up, they're gonna be sniffing around us soon enough."

"They ain't kids," says Josh.

"City-folk say they are," says Thiago.

"City-folk have brains like armadillions."

"That ain't news," says West. "But they've also got police and checkpoints on city gates. So yeah, okay, we'll help you. But we're gonna have to be discreet, okay?"

"Sure, just take a few extra contracts to pass to us for ready cash. Other than that, we can simply offload meat and goods to you that you can barter to other hunters for what we need so your usual city buyers won't be recording any increase in what you bring in. And give us the fuel you buy in-city and top off yourself at camps or farms you're on friendly terms with. That discreet enough?"

From the readiness with which Josh reels off these suggestions I'm guessing he's either thought about this a lot already or such tactics aren't unknown among hunters trying to avoid the authorities.

"Just like old times, huh?" says West.

Josh shoots a look at the photo frame, his brow scrunching up.

"Well, I guess not quite." West sighs, also shooting a look that way. Then he glances at Harry and me. "We used to do this kinda thing sometimes, whenever Isaiah got nervous about the baby-snatchers. The Wilson 'Vi stayed out for a year and a half straight, once, with Technicolor re-supplying them. No wonder Josh turned out the way he—"

West breaks off. He's clearly talking about Josh's city-phobia, which I know by now is no minor little dislike he has, but a really major deal. I mean, he came out here *on his own* rather than stay in there more than five days in a row.

"What happened?" I ask to cover the awkward moment. From West's embarrassment and Josh's stiffness, Josh is a bit tired of having his weirdness thrown in his face, even by an old family friend.

"Oh, well, dunno if anyone was actually on alert for them that time," West hurries on, "but finally they left Josh with us out-city and took the 'Vi in for servicing. No one was interested, so they relaxed again."

Josh is right. These *are* old, good friends of his. A strong sense of relief grips me, that we're not completely alone in this.

Trilly gives a plaintive call from the rear pen, feeling left out, and Ed shifts Kiko to his shoulder in order to rise and peer through the observation hatch. "Nice little tri-calf," he says.

"Yeah, can you take her to the university for me?" asks Josh. "She can't stay in here. She's growing fast and we're running out of feed powder."

"Sure," says West, "but let us offer her to them well before you actually cancel your contract. Even if they've already turned us down, they'll get back in touch for sure and change it to a yes. Anyone starts checking up on us, it'll look less suspicious than us offering her just after you've cancelled."

"Sure."

Harry shoots a glum look at Trilly's pen. Josh has just started letting us go in and feed her, and it was Harry who named her. I guess he's wishing she didn't have to go. I kinda feel the same way, it's nice having young stock around, but Josh is right. She needs more space.

"You got any contracts we can take?" Josh asks. "Easy stuff, mind, they ain't fully trained yet."

West laughs at the indignant look on Harry's face. "That one looks up for a bit of foot patrolling or rex nesting, wouldn't you say?"

"'Up for' and 'ready for' ain't the same thing." Josh speaks dryly.

Technicolor roar with laughter, while Harry does his manly best not to glare at Josh, who notices and grins approvingly, eyes glinting.

When West gets his breath back, he says, "Well, we have a boring wildflower survey that you'll do better than us anyway. And an order for twenty small herbivorous mammals for a petting zoo, which'll be tedious but hardly dangerous. And a pet shop order for piranha'saurs. That's all we have that's suitable. Other than that, just do some hunting. Edmo liver is going for a good price, and fill up the freeze-drier with the meat too, since the wild-caught is selling well at the moment. And if you see any intact triceratops skulls, lash 'em to your roof. They're the latest thing in stage decorations for concerts or some-such."

"Right. Good. I was wanting a piranha'saur anyway, to start motion training. If we have a penful for a while, we can catch a different one each time."

"What's motion training?" asks Harry.

For some reason, Technicolor laugh their heads off at this innocent question.

"*Useful*," drawls Ed. "It's real useful, is what it is, if a rex ever sticks its head in your face. Isaiah sure had a good tale to tell about *that*. S'why he trained Josh up so hard."

"You happy to take zoo taming contracts?" asks Thiago, sticking to business, glancing from me to Harry.

"Sure," says Josh. "They ain't gonna wander into no velociraptor pen, and they'll graduate from piranha'saurs quick enough, I reckon."

"Uh, what?" I ask, my heart doing a *thunk* in my chest. "What do you mean, graduate from? What *is* this motion training?"

More laughter from Technicolor. Even Harry looks uneasy.

Josh grins. "Well, first you sit still and try not to trip the motion sensors. Next level, I walk a piranha'saur around you on a leash and you sit just as still."

"Even if it nips you a little," says Ed, in a spooky voice.

Josh doesn't dispute this, just rubs a tiny scar on the

side of his face and says, "And then we graduate to a velociraptor. Muzzled and claw-tipped, of course—at least until graduation day."

Implying that on graduation day he's gonna walk an *unmuzzled* velociraptor around us? "Are you kidding?"

Technicolor laugh still more. Josh just drops suddenly into an incredibly raptorish pose, his eyes locking with mine as he prowls forward, making soft velociraptor sounds that I'm sure have to do with hunting and eating me. I find myself holding completely still, even when he comes eye-to-eye with me. But suddenly he blinks and relaxes and is just Josh again.

"Oh, she's gonna be good at this," says West approvingly.

"Sure is," Josh says. "But see, Darryl, if I were a rex and I were this close...you'd be glad of that training, right? 'Cos of that quirk with their vision that stops them locking in on unmoving things as prey."

"Of course—but I don't want to give Harry back to Dad with half his face bitten off."

"It'll always be on a leash. And it'll only be a velociraptor."

Only? Josh really doesn't think like the rest of us. Even Technicolor grin at his casual words.

"Actually," says Ed, "the contract Exception Zoo mentioned to us was for a Dakota."

"Dakotaraptor?" Josh throws a look at his rear pen. "How old?"

"Very young, obviously, or it couldn't be zoo-tamed in a 'Vi." Ed jabs a thumb at West. "The boss was fine with them wanting to give the contract to you, naturally, but since you won't officially be available I expect he can secure it instead. And you can tame the critter for us and have the lion's share. Just don't let it eat those kids or the city-folk will totally lose their—" He breaks off with a glance at me, swallowing the last word.

"Yeah, we'll take it." A spark of eagerness gleams in Josh's eyes, no surprise to me after Rusty. "If it gets too big for the motion training we can defer graduation until the pen's free again. But grab the contract, quick, so we can take our pick of this year's chicks before they get too big to handle."

West nods. "I'll get it, easy. That zoo guy always acts like you must've rubbed off on us or some'at. But—" he grins again "—don't see why you need no velociraptor for graduation. Just don't brush your teeth for a few days, blindfold 'em, prowl around 'em talking raptor to 'em and breathing on 'em and stroking 'em with a nice sharp claw, and see if they move."

After experiencing how convincing Josh can be even when I can *see* it's him...I shudder. West's face crinkles up with silent laughter. But Josh waves the suggestion away, oblivious.

61

"Don't be silly. Of course we need a real 'un. But a young Dakota won't take long to tame."

West throws me a grin, and the talk turns to the practical details of how they'll support us. They arrange things with few words, quickly firming up the plan and using the console to send contracts across from Technicolor to the Wilson 'Vi. When that's done, they start to catch-up a bit, and to question Harry and me in more detail about our problems, expressing rough but sincere sympathy.

"Wouldn't be surprised if there weren't something slightly more to it, though," says West, eventually. "A totally, hundred percent random kidnapping, just for cash? What are the odds? So I'd keep thinking on it, were I you. There's gotta be something else."

My heart sinks at his words, though I'm unsure whether that's a rational reaction or not. Something else? What? What could *possibly* have made someone do this to Dad?

JOSHUA

Soon enough we're walking Trilly through to Technicolor's rear pen, and Harry and Darryl are trying to be tough grown-up hunters as they just act the same as I do, giving her a quick pat and wishing her well in her new home.

"Say," remarks Darryl to West, as we gather back at

the doors to say goodbye. "You haven't got any raptor heads on your spikes, now. Doesn't putting them up there on your roof attract every scavenger nearby?"

I smile, pleased she's starting to identify threats so easily. "They just do it now and then to impress people," I say. "Usually someone they hope to earn from. Ain't a good idea, though."

West grins. "We don't leave 'em up long."

"It's still dumb." Josh's disapproval just makes the three much older men laugh. "*We* don't even have any come-eat-us spikes, you might note."

Darryl grins approvingly at my words—Technicolor just laugh some more, though after a moment Ed gives his head a sad shake. "Yep, that's what Zech always called 'em," he sighs.

"Yeah, and if you end up face-to-face with him 'cos of them, he'll have the fun of telling you 'I told you so,'" I say dryly. But Ed, whose religious convictions are rather weaker than those of Thiago or West, just shrugs. Never mind. If Uncle Z and Dad never talked them out of their vanity spikes (that was *Dad's* name for them), I'm not gonna manage it.

After a few goodbye back slaps, Darryl detaches Kiko from Ed, and they go into their 'Vi while we withdraw into ours.

"Josh," says West, his hand hovering over the door 'close' button, "watch yourself, okay? Don't let them catch you. You won't like it if they do."

63

I give him a reassuring nod. For a moment, I think he's going to add something else, then he grimaces and lets the door close. Soon they're heading off. No, I sure don't plan on letting 'them' catch us. I don't want no city-folk lecturing me and stealing my hard-earned savings for fines or threatening to take away my 'Vi-park license.

"Good," I say, when Darryl and Harry give me inquiring looks. "Now we've got support, ears, and contracts. We're set. Let's get to work."

The idea of getting to do some actual work makes Harry break out in a massive grin, and even Darryl looks excited. I smile back and go to the console to take a closer look at our new contracts.

HARRY

Well, I got excited way too soon about these contracts. The wildflower survey is dull as ditchwater, though Josh and Darryl seem to find it interesting. Since I'm so obviously 'not into this' Josh sticks me in the turret to provide cover, while they randomly toss a hoop a set number of times in each mountain meadow we stop at, before photographing every flowering plant inside where it lands and taking samples, all of which they painstakingly document once they're back inside. Booooring.

The mammals are a little more interesting, though it

takes a week to catch a full twenty and then they need constantly feeding and watering and cleaning out. But I haven't seen all the things Josh ends up with before. Many new variations of small mammal flourish nowadays, their size keeping them safe from large carni'saurs. Josh secures three separate species of squirrel—mountain, forest, and river—four kinds of mice, three types of those not-rabbit, not-rat kinda critters, five types of weasel or polecat, a miniature mountain fox, two distinct breeds of feral pre-restoration cats, and, last of all, a rat and a river shrew.

He catches most of them in cage traps, but they have to be checked really often so nothing comes along and smashes the trap to eat the critter inside before we can secure it. But the biggest challenge is simply housing them all in the 'Vi. Fortunately Josh has a bunch of little collapsible cages that he sets up, and the more laid-back of the herbivores get to wander around the rear pen in the space leftover, so long as they don't fight with each other.

All the predators are placed in individual cages and put together inside the second of the 'Vi's two big built-in critter cages, just in case they escape and try to eat the rest of the petting zoo's order. Josh warns us that feral cats may look like modern farm cats, but are wild as bobcats or pumas, and after collecting a nasty scratch trying to make friends with the sleek black one, I take him at his word and keep my hands to myself.

Ignoring his own advice, he sets to work taming the collection, and has soon stroked the cat that scratched me. One of the squirrels sits still while he teases a sticky spikey burr from its fluffy tail, and the fox yips excitedly when it's Josh who comes to feed it. Huh.

We acquired the piranha'saurs first thing of all, but that was kinda anti-climactic too.

"So, how do we catch them?" Yep, I had to go ask it so eagerly it made Josh laugh.

"Trust me, ain't no skill nor difficulty catching piranha'saurs," he replied.

And that certainly turned out to be true. He just found the right area, chucked some meat in the rear pen and dropped the access ramp. Soon enough a shoal appeared and flowed up the ramp and he closed the door. We then had to put on thick leather gloves and sort them, shoving the oldest and youngest and weakest back outside until we had enough good ones left to fill one of the two big built-in critter cages. They had to go in there, to make space for those twenty small mammals in the second cage and the rear pen. And that was all our contracts fulfilled, though we aren't meeting Technicolor again for over a week.

Since then it's been more learning and, finally, today, hunting. Even that was more work than glory. Josh let me drop the edmontosaur, but that bit was done ever so quickly. After that it was all blood and sweat as we butchered the beast, and that's a familiar enough chore from the farm, though normally you don't have to work top speed with the constant threat of scavengers larger and meaner than you requiring one person in the turret keeping watch.

We took the liver and the hide, then hauled one whole haunch inside the 'Vi to keep working on it. All the good meat from that went into the freeze-drier. We had to remove the rear pen's partition to fit the haunch into the vehicle and the small mammals spent the day stacked all around in every nook and cranny. Boy, were they in the way! I asked why we couldn't have hunted before catching them, but Josh said the meat would sell better if it was fresher, freeze-dried or no, and anyway, contracts first, always.

It all took *hours*. It took *all day*. And we had to work flat-out the whole time, because Josh said we weren't stinking of blood for a moment longer than necessary. Now we've finally hosed the 'Vi out I just want to flop, but Darryl is still unhappy at leaving all the rest.

"I guess if I'd thought it through, I'd've known hunters couldn't possibly carry off the whole animal," she's saying to Josh. "But it just seems so...wasteful. Shooting a critter and then not using all of it... It doesn't make me feel good at all."

Josh doesn't seem too worried by her farmer reaction. "Okay, let's get ourselves to a good observation point for the evening," is all he says. He drives us up to a 'bluff' with good visibility, and leaves

Darryl and me in the turret to watch the site of the kill while he puts some food on to cook. With my stomach aching and growling, I'm more interested in what he's doing down below than in the carcass, though I do know what Darryl means. But we've not eaten anything today other than a handful of dried fruit and nuts, gobbled standing up. Dad really did know what he was talking about when he said hunting was hard.

"Hey, look." Darryl elbows me.

I raise my binos and focus on the skinned, de-livered, de-haunched edmo. A pair of Utahraptors—the very largest raptor species, taller than a grown man—perch on top of it, heads dipping, gulping chunks of meat rapidly in between wary looks around.

"Where's the rest of the pack?" I say. The two mighty raptors are large adults but kind of thin and straggly looking.

Josh comes up the ladder and hands us each an apple. I barely manage to mutter "thank you" before biting into mine.

"There're only two Utahraptors there," I say, around my mouthful. "Where are the others?"

Josh takes a look with his binos. "Far away from here, I hope, for these two's sake. That's an old matriarch and her mate, eking out a precarious life on the fringes of other territories. Though right here ain't so fringe, but they smelled the meat. If they can fill their bellies before anything larger gets here, it'll do them a lot of good."

The Utahraptors successfully fend off the local family of deinonychuses, two cream and brown parents no taller than short women, with three fuzzy nestlings in tow, but finally break and run when an entire pack of Dakotaraptors arrives. The Dakotaraptors may be only man high, but they are many. They feast in turn, their feeding less frenzied than that of the larger raptor pair, more confident in their numbers and less hungry.

As the sun drops so low we can barely see, a bachelor pack of allosaurs arrives—large, boisterous, and dumb. They quickly drive the almost-sated Dakotaraptors away in turn. By this point, there's considerably less edmo meat down there.

The deinons still lurk, eyeing the kill, biding their time.

Josh gives Darryl an easy smile as he puts down his binos and lowers the turret's shutters for the night. "Well, it's too dark to watch longer. But take a look in the morning—and then we can have another chat about waste."

In the morning, a couple of little rodento'saurs are gnawing at the giant bones, teasing off the last scraps of meat.

"Yep," says Josh. "Just shoot one at a time, and nature don't really do waste."

"Do some hunters shoot more than one at once?" asks Darryl.

"Not meant to, but it's been known. Some guys were doing it so regular back when I were eight— several times we found these fields of stinking carcasses where they'd shot half a herd and just taken one prime part from each—it were real bad. No one liked it, but no one did nothing 'bout it, 'cos no one wanted to actually tell on them to DAPdep. Finally I got so fed up I slashed one of their tires one night in the 'Vi-park—and that takes some doing when you're eight, but I were that mad."

I whistle, thinking of the 'Vi's massive tires, and even Darryl looks impressed.

"Dad made me 'fess up and offer to pay," Josh continues, "but...well, I didn't do too good with the apology. Told 'em we'd cough up but kept calling 'em names. It just turned into a massive argument and every hunter in the park turned out to listen.

"Finally this old guy said no one would be offering them soil and leaf if they died if they carried on like that, which should've been a huge deal but...well, they didn't care because they were city-borns, so someone else said they'd lose their Vi-park license if DAPdep got to hear about it, and I guess that bothered them more. Seeing as 'most everyone was about mad enough at them by then to mebbe tell and not trying to hide it. Dad said afterwards that the other guys were all embarrassed a little kid had to act before they did. Anyway, the dud eggs went off to another state, so I dunno if they stopped. But they stopped doing it *here*, leastways."

I mean to ask about 'soil and leaf' but Josh has just started to talk about the plan for the day when Darryl says, "Josh— Uh, sorry, didn't mean to interrupt, it's just, I've been thinking..."

I forget all about 'soil and leaf' because I know at once from her tone that this is about Dad.

Josh clearly guesses too, because he says, "No worries, go ahead."

"Okay, well, I've been thinking really hard about this. We've got Technicolor listening out in the 'Vi-parks now. But what if the kidnappers contacted our neighbors? I think the other person I would really like to tell about all this is Father Ben. He could keep his ears open in our local area. If we tell *him*, we don't have to tell *everyone*."

Josh nods slowly. "I guess that makes sense. If you're sure you can trust him?"

"Oh, definitely."

"Absolutely!" I chip in. "Father Ben is the best."

"Okay. You'd better do it face-to-face, though. We don't want this bouncing around in messages."

I'm not sure, from his frown, if he's worried about kidnappers or the authorities intercepting it, but either might be bad, and Darryl's account number is floating around as common knowledge, now. I know he's using a ton of allusions and codewords to arrange things with

71

Technicolor, the advantage of their long friendship.

"Face-to-face? How will we do that?" I say.

A look of concentration settles on Darryl's face and she counts on her fingers. "I think I can still work out his schedule. Unless he's changed it, he'll be coming to the area to say Mass for the Wahlburgs in two Sundays' time. We've got a good chance of intercepting him somewhere on route."

"Good," says Josh. "We'll figure out a plan."

Darryl shoots a guilty look down through the hatch. "I can check with him about the Blessed Sacrament, too."

"What? What about It...er...Him?" asks Josh, who still seems very taken with his extra Guest.

"Well, a home tabernacle is a big privilege, you know. He might want to take the pyx back if he doesn't think ours is, y'know, good enough."

Josh looks so disappointed I'd be tempted to laugh if Darryl's words didn't make my own stomach swoop surprisingly low. Despite all the extra Adoration Josh's enthusiasm has us doing, having that tabernacle there makes the 'Vi feel so much like home. It *would* be a shame to lose it.

DARRYL

I lie with my nose in the dirt, barely daring to breath. Waiting. Still Josh doesn't speak from my earpiece. It's

72

never taken him this long to find me before. I really am improving. Satisfaction warms my chest, though my extremities remain cold and damp from hours of crawling through wet undergrowth. Along with motion training and actual work, Josh is still putting us through stalking exercises every few days.

Still nothing from Josh. Has my earpiece broken? I don't dare move to tap it, though. Or to actually hope he won't spot me in the end. He always does.

"Well," Josh's voice speaks at last, "we'd better get underway."

"Why," I ask. "Is there danger?"

"Nope, but this ain't a good spot for rabbits and we need to catch some if I'm to make pies for dinner."

"You can't find her!" whoops Harry from my earpiece, so loud I wince and barely manage not to move.

"Nope." I can picture Josh's laid-back smile. "I sure can't."

I'm so chilly I actually take a shower while we're moving, sliding around the tiny cubicle, chasing the soap as it skitters across the floor. By the time Josh pulls to a halt I'm still damp, but at least I'm now warm and in clean clothes. I collect my .22 and join them in the turret.

We're still in a rocky area, though the general dampness of the earlier terrain is now concentrated in small patches of bog and marshland circling the base of some outcrops, interspersed with larger areas of drier grass around others. It's in one of these slightly higher, drier patches that the rabbits have dug a warren, and as the 'Vi remains quiet and motionless they soon creep back out to nibble again.

Dusk is in the air; the colors beginning to fade. Still time for a quick rabbit hunt, though. After monitoring carefully for half an hour to be sure it will be safe to retrieve our catch, we all open fire at once, bagging a few rabbits each. A couple for tonight's pies, and some for the freeze-drier.

Josh offers to go out-vehicle, since he hasn't been lying in soggy undergrowth all day, so Harry and I prepare to cover him, swapping back to our normal rifles—Harry's is a .375 and mine's a .416—then rechecking the area and making another sweep with the drone.

"All good?" asks Josh from below.

"All good."

The side door hisses back and out he jumps, striding quickly across the open ground and stooping to start collecting up our dinner. I keep one eye on the drone's screens and one on the heat sensors, allowing only quick glances at what he's doing. But I still notice when he suddenly goes motionless, his head rising like he's practically scenting the air.

He drops the rabbits…

What the...

On the screen, a warm, *large*—oh Lord help, so large!—heat signature seems to appear from nowhere, only fifty feet up-slope...

JOSHUA

I couldn't honestly say precisely what tips me off, some combination of scent or sound or air currents or vibrations too subtle to pinpoint, but I sense the presence of a large predator with a certainty I don't stop to analyze. As Darryl blurts the codeword, "Red!" I've already dropped the rabbits, turned, and in one bound reached the closest patch of marsh. More like *puddle of marsh*, but I slide into it on my back, flat, hiding my face in a tiny patch of vegetation that allows me to keep my nose clear and breathe.

And see out. I wasn't a second too soon. Up-slope, an allosaur's head heaves into view. The ground shakes slightly as the huge predator lurches—limping badly—straight down to the warren, breathing raspily, pausing to give the 'Vi only the briefest wary glance before ducking its head to gulp the first rabbit.

Great. There go our pies.

Gulp.

Gulp.

Gulp.

Down they go. Please God, Darryl and Harry don't

75

panic and shoot the thing, 'cos it's so close it will probably fall on me and the only thing that can be said for having over two tons of allo land on you is that it's a very quick way to go. The threat from my inexperienced assistants aside, I'm not too worried. The chances of it scenting me in this bog are zilch. My heart rate is settling down now the first flush of adrenalin is fading.

Gulp.

Gulp.

Gulp.

A largish male, well past the age of being in any juvenile bachelor pack, the allo is gaunt and emaciated, and quite clearly starving. As it turns to grab the last couple of rabbits it's not hard to see why. A deep festering gash down its thigh, with a tell-tale crater of crushed, bruised flesh at one end, shows that it tangled with a fully-grown armadillion, or anchylosaur as their proper name is. More fool it. The spiked ball on the end of an armadillion's tail can cause a catastrophic injury even to a rex.

It shifts position to grab the final rabbit, staggering on softer ground. One foot slams down on the very edge of my patch of marsh. *Outage. Don't shoot, you two!* They might, if they think it's about to step on me...

Thankfully, they hold their fire. The lame allo has no wish to venture onto the even less stable terrain of my marshlet and gets itself back onto solid ground. After sniffing around for any missed rabbits, it begins to limp away.

I wait until it's got far enough that it won't easily pinpoint where the sound is coming from even if it notices before murmuring, "Darryl, drop the allo."

DARRYL

With the allo heading away, I'm relaxing slightly, beginning to re-check the screens, so Josh's quiet command takes me by surprise. "Uh...what? Right."

Quickly, I double-check my rifle-tip is through the bars, adjust my aim, and fire. Twice, because even my normal rifle is at the lighter end of things for taking out something this size, even with HiPiR rounds. Thankfully, both shots hit it square in the head and it lurches, staggers, and falls. The moment it's down, I put two more rounds into it, to be sure. The huge body twitches a bit from nerve spasms, but I think it's properly dead.

"Heck, where did that come from?" whispers Harry, sounding shaken.

Well, that's a Josh-level question. I don't know. I inspect the screens and the view from the windows as carefully as I can, while Harry does the same.

"Okay." I wish my voice didn't tremble slightly. "It's all clear, Josh."

If he made a snarky response I'd understand, but he just emerges from his marsh and heads back to the 'Vi looking muddy but perfectly relaxed.

77

As soon as the side door is closed again, I open the hatch, apologies on my lips, only to be hit in the face by a wave of bog stink. Josh stands just inside the door dripping ooze in a puddle all around him. He catches sight of his reflection in the window opposite and... laughs.

"Heck, I'm a swamp monster. Think you could just shut that hatch for a while, Darryl, so I can get straight in the shower and not track this into the cab?"

"Uh...sure." My apologies submerged by this onslaught of practicality, I close the hatch carefully and make sure the screens are all showing external camera feeds, then glance at Harry.

"Did he just walk back in here and laugh?" says Harry.

I shrug. "If you saw that too, then yeah, I guess he did."

"Huh."

HARRY

It's only about ten minutes before the hatch opens and Josh appears, de-swamped. He settles in one of the swivel seats, reaching for the drone controls and muttering, "That was interesting..."

"*Interesting?*" echoes Darryl. "Josh, I'm so sorry. I don't know how we could have missed something that big—"

He shoots her a look. "Hey, get that anguished look off your face. I missed it too, y'know? Call it, 'Why you always have cover when you go out-vehicle 101.'"

"102, surely," I can't help muttering. "I thought that ugly hole in your foot was lesson 101."

Josh shoots me just the hint of a glare for this, then shrugs. "Yeah, fair enough. Anyway, let's try and figure this out. The critter was so hungry it came for that food real fast, but it must've been close enough we should've seen it. But none of us did. I've got two thoughts..."

He swoops hither and thither with the drone, checking the landscape. "First thought," he says, "is that it was sheltering in a crack or gulley nearby. Almost certain."

"But you pointed the heat sensors into all of them, didn't you?" says Darryl.

"All that I *noticed*. I'm human, I could've missed one. But looking at this now—" he breaks off to tap a finger to the dead allo on the heat sensor screen "—that must've had a fairly cool signature for a live allo. Bordering on hypothermic with hunger, I'd say. If it were in a particularly deep crack, we coulda missed it more easily because of that. Hmm. *This* crack, maybe. Looks deeper than I realized the first time." He drops the drone lower, pointing the cameras directly at the ground, bits of shredded foliage flying from the rotors as he wriggles it right down below the level of the over-arching grasses. "Ah, yep...see that."

He's found an allo footprint.

"Should we have checked this low the first time?" asks Darryl.

"Well, no," says Josh. "Simply catching a few rabbits for dinner would have taken us half a day or more. The amount of time you spend checking corresponds largely to the amount of time you plan to spend out-vehicle, unless the terrain is utterly lethal. So we didn't really do anything wrong, y'see. This is just why you always have cover. Some hunters make the mistake of thinking that drones and heat sensors and stuff make them invincible. Ain't true. You've gotta have cover."

"Much use we were," I mutter. "If we'd shot it, it might've squashed you flat."

"True," said Josh. "But if it'd scented me, at that point it would've been far better for you to shoot than not, right? You understood that?"

"Yeah, of course."

"And if there hadn't been such good cover right there, you'd have shot it before it got to me, wouldn't you? So ignore the size and the big teeth, that wasn't a big deal."

"So we were right not to just shoot it on sight?" asks Darryl.

"Of course." Josh looks surprised. "There might not have been anything wrong with it, and I was safely hidden. Swamp, y'know, is a real God-send in that situation. Total scent-block. Though it does demand payment in blood, often as not. You should've seen the size of the leech I pulled off me in the shower."

"Yuck," says Darryl, as an "Ew" escapes from me too.

Josh just shrugs. "I'd rather get bit by a leech than an allo." He laughs again, then sighs. "Shame it ate our rabbits. Oh well. Let's grab a few photos of its wounds for the cull report before it goes totally dark. We can get the teeth and claws tomorrow. Nothing'll eat those."

Darryl and I are familiar with cull reports by now. With our lockers almost full of freeze-dried meat and our live capture capacity practically over-flowing, work for the last week has meant locating sick or injured 'saurs and putting them down, documenting everything so we can claim bounty from DAPdep—the Dinosaur Activity and Population department. Or rather, so Technicolor can claim it for us, minus a cut for their trouble. We've carefully collected up all saleable teeth, claws, feathers, bones, and horns, though the hide is usually a dead loss from cull animals. All of which has to be immediately cleaned of any gore, then put aside for further cleaning and polishing later.

Some hunters, Josh has explained, will be back in-city every week or two, off-loading meat and taking on contracts. The Wilson 'Vi has always specialized in contracts and work that doesn't require regular in-city visits, be it surveys, zoo-taming, general non-contract culling or handicraft making.

That's good news as far as I can see it. Not only is Josh already an expert at choosing the right work for our situation, but we won't be doing all that butchering more than once in-between each meeting with Technicolor. Because call me lazy, but that really was a lot of work—*and* it felt like there was a huge target painted on the 'Vi the whole time. Here, Rexy, Rexy! Big meal, here!

Which is why Josh insisted we remain parked fairly near the carcass even once we had our haunch inside. So that anything large enough to breach our armor would go for the more easily accessible meat first, thus giving us a chance to flee. I'd seriously never thought through how dangerous a *successful* hunt could be for the *hunters!*

Josh hums absent-mindedly as he manipulates the drone controls, positioning the camera. It's clear he really does regard what just happened as a very minor incident, like tripping and falling in a cow pat because a mare got into the wrong field. Even an allo is no big deal if you have good enough scentCam?

Guess Darryl and I still have a lot to learn.

JOSHUA

"What's this?" Darryl comes down from the turret one evening, a few days after we offloaded everything to Technicolor, and leans over my shoulder, peering at the feathers in my hands. We're gonna lie in wait for their parish priest in a week's time, so I want to get this project finished.

"It's a curtain for the tabernacle," I say, holding it up. "It's almost done. I thought we could make wall hangings, too. To make it more special."

It's just a simple bit of feather fabric, denser and more solid than lace, but Darryl exclaims over it in delight. It is multi-colored and shimmery. "That's great, Josh. Can you show me how to make one?"

"Sure."

Over the next few evenings, Harry and Darryl both make a square of sleek feather fabric, hoping to contribute. They don't do badly for a first try, but they decide for themselves that it ain't good enough for the tabernacle. So I make three more squares and decorate the tops with a little border of teeth. Darryl seems quite alarmed when I suggest the teeth, but once I've started adding the row of tiny dainty canines, she relaxes. Guess she thought I meant something large and tasteless.

Unfortunately, once the hangings are all installed, I can't think of a single other thing to do to make the explosives box a more honorable berth. We'll just have to hope it's enough.

DARRYL

Little did I know how soon I'd need my new skills! I'm lying hidden in a—fortunately dry—section of drainage ditch beside the minor road that winds through the wilderness to connect the main highway to Exception City with the cultivated area where our farm lies nestled between Maurice Carr's and the Wahlburgs' holdings. The 'Vi is parked behind some outcrops a short distance from the road. Josh and Harry have a clear view over them from the turret, but a camo net makes sure it's not visible from the road.

My back's starting to ache. I've been in this ditch for almost three hours. No sign of Father Benedict's van yet. Shiny and black, with a white dorsal stripe from front to rear like a vehicular clerical collar, it would be hard to miss. If he doesn't come along soon, maybe I can swap with Harry and take a stint monitoring for danger.

So far the only thing that's happened was Josh telling me to stay particularly still and quiet for a while because some deinons were prowling a quarter mile away and somewhat later he had me roll into the shelter of an outcrop while a herd of iguanodons wandered through nearby.

The only thing, huh? I guess I really am getting used to life out here.

If my back wasn't so sore, I'd probably be nodding off, here in the sun...

"Darryl? SOS van inbound."

Finally! Father Benedict hasn't changed his schedule. Good. I get to hands and knees and peep out of the ditch. I can see dust—the drizzle of last week has been replaced by a real foretaste of summer—but no vehicle. Ah, there. Once the van comes into sight, I straighten and climb up onto the side of the road. No need to wave. The van is already screeching to an abrupt halt, the window sliding down.

"*Darryl?* Thank God! Get in, quickly! Are you alright?"

I go up to the window, but don't get in. I don't *think* he'd drive off with me for my own good, but he is city-born, though an honorary country-dweller after all these years.

"Relax, Father Ben," I say quickly. "I'm quite okay, I've got cover. I was just waiting for you to come along."

"Well, I'm here, thank goodness, so get in! Where's Harry? *Is he okay?*"

"He's fine. It's all okay. Can you just follow me around behind that outcrop over there? The ground's solid. Then we can have a cup of Joe and a chat."

Father Ben's eyes narrow. "Hmm. All right. But for

pity's sake, *get in*."

"No, I'll just show you the way." I head off before he can argue. Cautiously, he drives off the road behind me, but the van bounces easily over the low scrubby grassland. We get behind the shielding outcrop before any other vehicles come. No surprise, for such a quiet minor road, but still a relief.

Once Father Ben's parked close beside the 'Vi, Josh's voice comes from the van's interCar as he sticks to standard procedures: "Black SOS van, you're clear to come over to the HabVi."

"Am I," mutters Father Ben...blackly. Oh dear. Nope, he doesn't seem too happy as he opens his door and gets out. He's like a small dark thundercloud behind me.

But once we're inside the 'Vi and the door slides closed, he looks around, then turns to give me a quick, tight hug, before pushing me away to look me up and down. "Oh, Darryl, are you okay? I'm so sorry about Carol... I'm so glad you're *safe*..." He looks around as Harry appears on the ladder from the turret. "And *Harry*...thank God."

Harry gets enfolded in a hug as soon as he reaches the bottom. "Where have you two been—" he cuts himself off, glancing around the 'Vi "—well, that much is obvious. Oh, hello Kiko."

Kiko gets some attention, though more absent-minded than usual, then Father Ben's gaze snaps to Josh

86

as Josh slides down in turn.

"And *you*—" Father Ben pulls a tire iron from his trouser waistband, holding it at the ready "—what do you think you're playing at, making off with these kids like that?"

When did he grab *that*? I don't think he's allowed to hit anyone with it, so I guess he's bluffing. Maybe not a smart move…

But Josh's eyes widen as they fall on Father Ben, and he grins, ignoring the makeshift weapon.

Father Ben's eyes widen too. "Hey!" The tire iron droops, too late to stop Kiko retreating to my shoulder instead. "You're the boy who had the allo in his jacket! You're *that* Joshua!"

Allo in his *jacket*?

"And you're *that* Father Ben!" says Josh, nothing but delight and welcome on his face. "Thanks again for your help back then. It's real nice to meet you again."

Father Ben's brows draw together, as though he's not sure he shares the sentiment, his grip tightening again on the metal in his hand as he glances warily around the vehicle. "Where's your uncle? Is Zechariah here?"

Josh's face tightens, and he shakes his head. Father Ben lets out a pained breath, some more of his anger draining away, his knuckles relaxing again. "Ah, no. Not him too?"

Josh just nods, mutters, "Heart attack," then turns

87

and starts lining up mugs on the pull-out work-top, shoulders hunched.

Father Ben lets out a big, big sigh, shoves the tire iron back through his belt and runs his hands through his tightly coiled black hair. His eyes dart from me to Harry. "So, *have* you been kidnapped?"

"What? *No!*" Harry and I speak on top of each other.

"Of course we haven't!" I say. "We *chose* to come with Josh. *We* suggested it."

"We're *working* for Josh," says Harry. "We're his assistants. He's training us real good."

"*You* suggested it. Right." Father Ben rakes his fingers through his hair some more. "Well, that *is* what Maurice said. That you'd just skipped out because you didn't want to go in-city. That Fernanda lady was telling a rather different story. The way she told it, you'd have thought she'd heard you screaming in the night as the ruthless hunter lad forced you into his vehicle at gunpoint and made off with you."

"What?" I shriek, outraged on Josh's behalf. "Is she *telling* people that?"

"Not quite in so many words, but near enough. Wanted the army sent after you, helicopters, the works. Thankfully, with Maurice and Riley telling such a different story, and Maurice with that message from you for some sort of proof, they haven't been very interested. But the police and the CPS *are* interested.

Very. You need to give yourselves up, Darryl, Harry, before you get Joshua in any worse trouble." He looks from one to the other of us, very sternly.

"You don't understand," I say quickly, as Harry shoots me an imploring glance. "It's *not* just about us not wanting to live in-city. It's about *Dad*. We've got a lot to tell you. That's why we needed to speak to you."

"About your *dad?*" Father Ben's eyes narrow. Abruptly, he pulls back a nearby chair and sits in it, leaning forward, elbows on his knees. "Okay, I'm listening. What about your dad?"

I tell him, trying to make it all as clear and rational as possible, as Harry blurts out extra details here and there. Josh calls up our 'crime scene' photos on the console screen and points out some of the most obvious flaws in the 'animal attack' theory. Father Ben listens hard, thank God, and doesn't immediately tell us it's just some childish fantasy we've come up with because we don't want to believe Dad's dead.

"Not dead but kidnapped," he says slowly, at last. "That's really what you think?"

"Not killed *then*, I *know*," says Josh firmly. "Not killed then by a carni'saur, I *know*."

"The rest *is* speculation," I say. "But it makes sense, right? Why not kill him right there or leave him outside the fence to be eaten right away? Kidnap has to be the most likely."

"And that's why you've gone on the run with
89

Joshua?"

"Well, we thought we were just coming to work for him. But since the city-folk are overreacting, I guess we're on the run."

Okay, deep down, we knew they might. That's why we fled so far, so fast, the first night. But it's still hard to believe they can make so much fuss about it.

"We *have* to stay free," says Harry, "so the kidnappers can arrange an exchange! If we go in-city, they'll kill Dad!"

Father Ben grimaces, but doesn't disagree. Point to us. Surely he'll help?

"We need you to listen out on the farm side of things," I say quickly. "Just in case they contact Uncle Mau or Riley and Sandra instead of messaging us directly. I mean, no guarantee that messaging number of mine will end up in their hands, despite our best efforts."

Still Father Ben says nothing.

"Father Ben, you've *got to help*," I say. "Don't you understand how serious this is?"

"That's the problem," he says grimly. "I do see how serious it is. But I don't think you three understand how serious your own situation is. Darryl, as the older sibling, and the instigator, well, your chances of not ending up in juvie will drop the longer this goes on. They're probably low enough already. Harry's younger so he'll probably just be put with a foster family under

90

close supervision. But Joshua is an adult, and he'll stand trial for this as an adult."

"Stand trial?" All the hairs on my back prickle coldly. "What do you mean? Won't they just fine him or tell him off or something?"

Father Ben's face remains unyieldingly grim. "Joshua is eighteen, an *adult*. You and Harry are not. You are *minors*. He is not your parent or guardian. He has no legal authority over you, no legal right to take you anywhere, much less into employment in his rather dangerous trade. *Legally*, he *has* kidnapped you. Now, if the judge believes you when you say this was all at your instigation, it might only be classed as felony kidnapping, which means kidnapping under the legal definition only, not in reality. But, with minors, it still carries a term of at least one or two years. But if Fernanda has her way—well, for normal kidnapping the minimum term is twenty years."

Twenty years. There's a strange buzzing in my ears. What have we done? My eyes feel impossibly wide as I glance at Josh. He's frozen, not even breathing, as though the 'Vi door is open and he's sensed another allo peeping in.

"*Term?*" He speaks at last, his voice strangled. "What do you mean, *term?*"

"Term of imprisonment." Father Ben's voice is soft now. "I'm sorry, Joshua, but they will send you to prison for this."

JOSHUA

My back's flat to the wall; I'm wedged right in the corner. I can't breathe properly and my head rings, my vision blurring, like when I've stayed in-city too long, 'cept I've never felt like this when just standing in the 'Vi. I fight to control my breathing, to speak.

"They...they can't do that! I ain't...I ain't *done nothing!*"

"You have. In their eyes, you have." From Father Ben's grim tone, he maybe agrees with them, at least a little. "You can't just take two kids and waltz off with them. Especially into this sort of danger."

"Danger? I rescued them! They wanted to come... I ain't done nothing!"

The priest sighs, unbending a little. "Well, since when did that stop hunters landing in jail?"

Unfortunately, he's right. City courts always think the worst of us. Nausea churns in my stomach and my balance still feels off. I can't catch my breath. I want to run. And run. And run. Until the sky opens out and I can breathe again. Except the sky outside the 'Vi is already open. It's like the city has reached all the way here and is squeezing me to death.

"You need to breathe, Joshua. You don't look good."

I lay my cheek to the cool metal of the nearest cupboard-front and close my eyes. I ain't in-city, so I don't know how to stop this. I can't just get away, like I normally would.

Saint Des, help me! Dad, help!

Uncle Z,

Pray for me!

That little rhyme usually makes me smile, but not now.

"Try to relax, Joshua," the priest persists. "I can't imagine Fernanda having her way of it with a court. If they get the kids back safe and sound and...well, sound..." I think he glances at Darryl then, though I'm not sure why, "then there's no way she's getting a normal kidnapping charge to stick. So no way would it be twenty years. And if you took them straight back now and apologized, cut some deal with them...well, I guess it's just possible it wouldn't see the inside of a courtroom."

"Deal?" breaks in Darryl, her voice thin. "How could Josh make a deal? That's what criminals do, isn't it, ratting each other out?"

She's right. I've nothing to trade to the police. I just can't breathe. Heck, am I gonna pass out? Everything's going grainy, now...

"Hey, you've got to calm down, Joshua." The priest has come to my side, gripping my arm. "I think you're having a panic attack. You've just got to breathe. I shouldn't have mentioned twenty years at all. No way it'll be more than one or two."

I rip my arm from his grip, spin and slam a fist into

the nearest metal surface. "One or two *years*? In-city? And you dare tell me to *relax?*"

I slide sideways, back flat against the side door. My groping hand finds the door controls, the possibility of escape, and suddenly I can breathe again. A little. I don't press the button—but I could.

"They can say what they like about me," I snap. "Make their court decisions. If they actually turn up here and try to take me, then I'm out this door and gone. Let them hunt me through the wilderness on foot, if they want me that much."

My vision clears enough I can see three faces staring at me, two pale, one dark, all wearing identical expressions of horror.

"Josh," whispers Darryl, "you'd never survive!"

"Something would eat you for sure!" cries Harry.

I tilt my head back against the door, closing my eyes to block it all out, tracing the soothing shape of the button under my finger. Freedom... "Oh, I lived out there for over a week, one time. You can bet I'd manage a month, no problem."

"A month?" explodes the priest, sounding outraged. "You'd trade the entire rest of your life for a *month?*"

"To avoid a year in-city?" I open my eyes again, drop my chin and glare at him. "In a heartbeat. Anyway, Saint Des managed a *lot* more than a month. Mebbe I would to."

"Joshua..." Darryl stares imploringly at me. "You can't be serious?"

The priest's gaze is starting to carry a whole different level of concern. "Are you *actually* crazy?" He glances at Darryl and Harry, like he thinks he really does needs to remove them from my care.

"No, he's not!" flares Darryl. "He's got super-bad city-phobia, is what, if you'd take the trouble to find out! This is *huge* deal for him!"

"And you think a *year* in prison is 'oh, relax' for anyone?" snaps Harry.

It warms my uneasy gut to hear them defending me, but now that the worst of the attack has passed off I feel weak and shaky. I slide down, my back still to the door, my legs spread out over the floor, and stare up at them as I draw in breaths.

After a moment, Darryl plunks herself in front of me, staring intently.

"Josh..." Harry tenses as she speaks in a low voice as intent as her gaze, but keeps silent. "If you want to turn us in...this is no way what we thought we were asking of you. It's okay if you do..."

"And what about your dad?" I speak in just as low a voice.

She winces, her face screwing up in anguish.

"No," I say. "This don't really change anything. Your dad still needs rescuing. Once we've got him back, he can give me, like, retroactive permission and square things with the city-folk. And in the mean time, it's real simple. We cannot let ourselves be caught. End of discussion."

HARRY

I don't want to say anything that might change Josh's mind, but I can't help whispering, "But what if we *can't* get Dad?"

Josh shrugs. "When Darryl's eighteen I can just skip off to another state if necessary. Guess we could do that anyway, if we despair of getting your dad…"

"No!" breaks in Father Ben. "*Don't* do that. Not with them in tow. I'm not a lawyer, but I'm pretty sure crossing state lines with them will complicate things ten times more, legally speaking."

"Oh." Josh peers up at the priest tiredly. "Okay."

Silence settles over the 'Vi. Darryl still peers anxiously at Josh, and Father Ben keeps biting his lip, opening his mouth, shutting it again, and biting his lip some more.

Since Josh got called to explain the photos before he could actually make the drinks, I move over to the worktop and take care of it. I put a big gob of honey into Josh's, though he doesn't usually have any, 'cos he still looks kinda grey and shaky. Panic attack? Is that what happens to him when he goes in-city? It looked nasty. Here I was thinking Josh wasn't scared of *anything*. He murmurs a sincere-sounding "thank you" when I hand him the tea and sips without any comment on its sweetness.

"Okay," says Father Ben at last, looking up from what's left of his own tea with a slight sigh. "The decision about whether to stay out here, I think, has to belong to you three. The consequences are far too serious for me to make it for you, when you're all mature enough to decide for yourselves."

He shoots me an uneasy look, like he's unsure if he should be including me in that, but simply goes on, "If you choose to give yourselves up, I'll speak for the good intentions of all concerned as best I can and be what help I can. If you decide to stay out here, I'll put my ear to the ground around all the farms I visit and see if I can hear anything about your dad. I don't see what more I can do."

"You can promise not to tell anyone where we are or that you met us." Josh speaks from where he still sits at the base of the side door.

Father Ben looks exasperated. "I *think* that goes without saying."

Josh shrugs. "Sorry, Father. You've made me a tad jittery."

"Fair enough." Father Ben sips more tea, then looks up suddenly. "Oh, Darryl, on the subject of missing things...after I heard what happened I swung by the Franklyn farm as soon as I could to collect the pyx, but it wasn't here. Please tell me you have it safe?"

"Of course," says Darryl. I can tell she's trying not to sound too worried as she goes on, "We've made a really nice tabernacle here in the 'Vi. We were hoping you could inspect it and tell us if it was okay."

"You mean, okay to *keep* it?"

Darryl nods, as Josh and I watch intently. She rushes on, "We've been having Adoration. I think I've been doing everything just right. I hope that's okay. You did say we could..."

"You've been having Adoration." He looks from one to the other of us, shaking his head wonderingly under our anxious gazes. "Three teenagers in the middle of nowhere have been devoutly having Adoration, while a brother priest in one city-parish I know of struggles to round up three parishioners. Huh."

He dismisses this with one more shake of his head and directs a sympathetic look from one to the other of us. "Well, of course I'll take a look, but don't get your hopes up. Home tabernacles have to be suitably secure and sanctified spaces, you know." He glances around at the utilitarian metal of the 'Vi and winces. "So, uh, I'm guessing I will have to take the pyx away with me."

Darryl's unlocking the gun cabinet and beckoning Josh to his feet to open the explosives box, since his explosives license doesn't cover us having access to that.

"Sanctified means, like set aside and special, right?" she says hopefully. "Well, we've made it really special. And you can see how *secure* it is."

Father Ben winces again. "There is no way the bishop is going to be satisfied with a pyx simply locked up in a gun cabin—" He breaks off, eyes widening, as Josh swings open the little door to reveal the shimmering feather curtain, decorated with two little crosses made from those dainty little teeth. "Well, that's...that's nicer than I expected."

Josh and I kneel down as Father Ben genuflects and steps forward to gently move the curtain aside and look in, but Darryl hovers at his side for another moment, filling him in in an undertone as to the preciousness of the simple shirt carpeting the 'tabernacle' before dropping to her knees herself. We wait breathlessly as Father Ben peers around inside our tiny sacred space for a while.

"So, uh," his voice comes slightly muffled. "What are these blocks under here?"

"C4 and dynamite, mostly." Josh sounds nervous. "I really ain't got nowhere else to keep them."

"Hmm. More hangings on the walls. Huh, featherlace corporeal. That's real nice." Finally, with one more "Hmm," he genuflects again and swings the door shut. "Well," he says, "the bishop is supposed to approve home tabernacles, y'know. And there are obvious reasons why I can't exactly mention this to him just yet. So I probably ought to take it. But you've certainly done your very best and it's not half bad. Let's just say if I forgot to collect the pyx before I left, I wouldn't lose any sleep about it being looked after properly."

Is he saying...? No one seems to want to ask him straight out—and I guess he probably doesn't want us to.

We have another cup of Joe, and Father Ben gives us his schedule for the next month or two so we can intercept him again. Josh also works out a bunch of code phrases with him that he can message back and forth to Darryl's account without giving anything away. Father Ben also assures us he's already said several Masses for Dad and for Carol. He'll change the ones for Dad to 'Masses for One in Peril' in future, he adds. But, right now, he needs to get on his way so no one will notice the delay in his journey.

"Oh, Gold's in Exception Zoo, now," calls Josh from the turret, once we're satisfied all's clear—'saurs and other vehicles both—and Father Ben's about to move back to his van. "She's a real fine lady, now."

"Gold?" Father Ben looks puzzled for a moment, then his brow clears even as Josh calls, "Y'know, the one you stroked. She still likes me a lot, thank Saint Des."

Father Ben grins. "Well, maybe I'll go see her some time. Okay, well, I'm off. For goodness' sake, be careful, you three."

"Of course we will," Darryl and I chorus.

Shooting worried looks back at us, he blesses us and climbs out. But at the last moment, he beckons Darryl and when she crouches down to get her head level with his, he speaks softly to her. I barely catch it.

"Darryl, there is one thing that could make things *much* worse for Joshua and I'm sure you can guess what it is. Don't let it happen."

Darryl frowns fiercely at him. "Is that what you think of me?"

"No, it isn't, or I wouldn't be going along with this. But that boy's up to his neck in hot water already, quite apart from the obvious objections. Just bear it in mind."

With that, he gives her an extra blessing, ignoring her scowl, and gets into his van.

"What was that about?" I ask Darryl, as soon as she's closed the door.

"Nothing," she says.

Soon Father Ben's back on the main road, driving away. Josh heads straight down to the cab to get us underway too. I'm not sure if he doesn't entirely trust Father Ben, or if the last hour has just left him super-paranoid. Either way, we're immediately heading back towards wilder expanses, keeping off-road.

"So, did you notice?" says Darryl a few minutes later, as she settles in the cab with me and Josh and hands out some snacks.

"He didn't take the pyx?" I say.

"Yep."

She half-heartedly high-fives me when I raise my hand, and even sober-faced Josh almost smiles, though it doesn't make it into his eyes. Momentarily buoyed by this good news, I ask, "Josh, why did you have an *allo* in your jacket?"

"How did it *fit*?" asks Darryl.

Josh almost-smiles again. "Well, it were only a little one. It were two Christmases ago. My Uncle Z and I were up in Tana State for a Christmas break..."

He tells the story—and what a story!—but without quite his usual enthusiasm, and once he's finished we mostly travel in silence. When Josh finally stops five hours later, he goes up into the turret without any dinner and shuts the hatch behind him. According to the "Vi-rules' he taught us, that means he doesn't want company. It's the first time he's ever done it. He must be feeling bad.

Darryl and I nibble at a light meal in a sick silence, struggling to find words to say to each other. How can things be this serious? It's so crazy.

We turn in soon afterwards, but I stare up into the darkness of my bunk for a long time, thinking about Josh locked up in prison, clawing at his throat, unable to breath. Of Josh, running through the undergrowth, cops and raptors on his trail...

And about how it's all our fault.

DARRYL

I sleep fitfully for a while, then I end up wide awake and I can't manage to settle off again. Eventually I give up and turn the light up just slightly. Kiko is sleeping, his head tucked under one forewing-limb, so I climb quietly down from my berth. I'll get a hot drink, maybe sit in the turret for a while and pray or read my handpad.

Prison. Why, Lord? It's not fair. He's only trying to help us!

When I glance up at the turret as I move to the boiler tap, the hatch is open. Oh? If Josh had gone to bed, he'd have closed it. A breeze ruffles my hair—the turret windows are open. Josh is still up there. I hesitate, but...the hatch is no longer locked—or even closed.

I make a second hot drink, then carry them both in one hand while I climb the ladder. Yep, Josh is still there, leaning on the console with his chin on his folded arms, face inches from the open window. The moon's so bright I can see the breeze playing with his hair too, and for a moment he looks like a lion staring out of the bars of a cage.

Then he glances at me and offers, if not a smile, a welcoming expression. I hold out the mug. He uncoils

103

and accepts it. For a while we sip in silence, but then I have to say it. Dad would understand.

"Josh, I really do mean it when I say…if you don't want to do this, you can drop us by the side of a highway for highway patrol to take in-city, and you can go out-state. This isn't something we can ask of you."

"I know you ain't asking, okay?" he says softly. "But you don't always do a thing because you've been asked. Sometimes a thing is right and best. Sometimes in more than one way."

"As long as you're really sure. That it's right and best."

"If I give you two up, your dad will die. That's enough. And you two will be stuck in-city, and—" he finishes so softly I strain to catch the words "—and I'll be alone again."

He straightens his shoulders and sips his coffee, finally shedding some of his gloom. "We'll just keep a real low profile," he says firmly. "Make sure they don't catch us."

I eye his face in the bright moonlight. Did anything we said have any impact on him?

"And if…?"

"And if they do catch us?" His voice goes resolute as the granite on which we're parked and the wildness in his eyes makes him look a part of the wilderness behind him.

No, and nothing we say will...

"If they catch us—" no bluff or bravado in his eyes, just simple truth "—I'll run."

==+==

Don't miss unSPARKed 6!
A Right Rex Rodeo

MANDY LAMB AND THE FULL MOON

CAN A HALF-SHEEP GIRL AND A WEREWOLF BE FRIENDS?

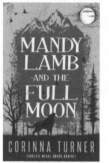

Mandy Lamb is the world's only half-sheep girl, thanks to a spot of well-meant but ill-advised genetic tinkering. She's starting senior school and she's about to meet James, a strange, dog-like orphan who has a bad habit of running off at the full moon. With danger on the way, will James prove friend or foe?

This page-turning rural fantasy is a heart-warming tale about friendship, trust, and courage—and not letting what you are define what you do. Those looking for a unique, challenging read will love this 'animal yarn with a Christian twist.'

-+-

"CORINNA TURNER takes Urban Fantasy to the countryside with the adventures of a half-sheep girl who is up for befriending anyone—even a werewolf or a vampire! A hilarious twist on familiar tropes that all ages will enjoy."
ELIZABETH AMY HAJEK, author of *The Mermaid and the Unicorn.*

"A book about fitting in despite your uniqueness and accepting others for who they are, with all of their gifts and challenges. It also delivers a firm message about distinguishing dispositions (which we cannot help) and actions (which we can) …
Overall, a fun story about friendship with a pulse-pounding climax and an element that resonates in every story—self-sacrifice."
AN OPEN BOOK FAMILY

READ ON FOR A SNEAK PEEK

The boy dropped over the high stone wall and landed lightly on his feet. He remained motionless for a moment, listening, then eased through the shrubbery until he could peep out. Round the front of the house he could just see a woman standing next to a car. He could hear her tapping her nails impatiently on the hood. He had very good hearing.

"Well?" the woman asked, as a man hurried out to join her. "Where is he?"

"There's a rolled-up blanket in his bed. Didn't you check last night?"

"*No*, I didn't check. It's about his 'time of the month', isn't it? Do you think he chooses the full moon specially, just to wind us up?"

The boy loped across the lawn and let himself in quietly at the back door.

The woman went on, "I'm sick and tired of phoning the police only to have him come strolling back in time for breakfast. Quite frankly, I've reached the point where I'd rather not know if he's taken himself off for a bit. But *today*? He seemed so keen on the idea of a fresh start!" She heaved a big sigh. "Well, I know he's missing now. I shall have to phone the police."

She swung around and started—the boy stood behind her. He had a rucksack on his back and a water-filled plastic bag in his hands with a big black goldfish swimming around inside.

"*There* you are!"

"You haven't been waiting long, have you?" asked the boy politely.

The woman made an exasperated noise and opened the car door. "Come on, get in, then."

The boy didn't move.

"What?"

"You haven't yelled at me yet."

The woman shook her head. "Oh no, James, in a few hours when we reach Wales you'll be someone else's problem and I shall let them waste their breath. In you get, now."

The boy shrugged, slipped off the rucksack and stuffed it in the back as she got into the driver's side. He settled into the passenger seat and put the fish on his lap.

She glanced at him. "Is that everything?"

"It's all I want."

"Well, be careful with that fish."

"I'm always careful with my fish," said the boy, flatly.

The woman glanced at him again, but stuck the key in the ignition rather than reply.

The man looked through the car window. "Bye, James. The new place sounds nice. Try to make it work, won't you?"

The boy nodded his dark head sadly. "I'll try."

1

Mandy stuffed a wad of juicy clover flowers into her mouth and chewed happily. She reached out a hand for more, but the village clock began to chime in the distance.

It couldn't be that time already!

She released the fistful of flowers she had been about to pluck and tried to care that she was going to be late. It was hard. But she knew Ricky's dad was a busy man, like most farmers, so she started running, racing across the field, her little tail frisking behind her.

Despite what awaited her at the Fletchers' farm, she couldn't feel gloomy on a day like today. Soft, green grass bent under her hoofy toes, and her fleece—still short from shearing—left her cool and comfortable in the late summer sunshine, though it grew long at the bottom, falling to her knees like a thick woolly skirt.

Her wool was also a little itchy, so her more rational side wasn't sorry that she was on her way to Mr. Fletcher's. Her more rational side had little chance of winning in a situation like this, though.

She found herself slowing to a walk again.

She probably didn't even have any lice. This probably wasn't really necessary. Except...

Except she started her new school tomorrow. Secondary school in the nearby town of Treflan. And she wanted to look really, *really* clean and...well, *sanitary* when she met all her classmates-to-be.

Her new school. Mandy's stomach sank a little, despite the sunshine, and she glanced from her arms—as pale and human as those of any local girl—to her woolly body. How would a half-sheep girl like herself fit in?

She comforted herself by eating the dandelion still clenched in her hoofy fingers and forced herself to run again. She'd be able to see the Fletchers' farm from the top of the next rise. And Ricky would be there, and he was her best friend in the village. It wouldn't be so bad.

Then she heard the screaming. Most people would only have heard bleating, not even hearing the fear in it. But to her it sounded like screaming.

She skidded to a halt so fast her little hoof-toes scored the ground. Snatching up a nearby stick as a concession to the fact that she was just a little girl, and a part-sheep girl at that, she ran towards the screaming as fast as she could. Clearing a stone fence in one leap, she found what was—to anyone with one drop of sheep DNA—a scene of utter terror.

Sheep fled wildly in all directions, trying to avoid being trapped in the field corners by the big black dog that sought to catch them.

"House-wolf! House-wolf!" came the panic-stricken bleats. "Run! Run! House-wolf!"

"Sheep! Sheep!" barked the dog, slathering with excitement. "Oh, oh, it's so exciting. Sheep! Sheep! They smell so good! I've gotta catch one! I've gotta catch one! Ooh, they smell good..."

The sight of such a big, snarling dog made most of Mandy want to turn and run away bleating "house-wolf" as well.

"Maaandy! Maaandy, run!" bleated the nearest sheep as they fled past her. "House-wolf, Maaandy. Run!"

She resisted the temptation to take this advice and dashed forward. Even as she did so, the dog bore down on a tiny little lamb that had fallen over itself in its haste to flee.

"No!" gasped Mandy, but she was far too far away. The dog leaped...

"GET AWAAAY FROM MY LAAAMB!" A very small ewe flew into the dog at full speed, knocking it to the ground before its jaws could close around the lamb. "GET AWAAAY! GET AWAAAY!"

"Acorn!" gasped Mandy, still running flat out.

"GET BAAACK!" bleated the little ewe, standing between the dog and the lamb, which was finally getting back to its tiny hooves. "STAAAY BAAACK OR I'LL HURT YOU!"

The dog rolled onto its feet, snarling in embarrassment, and immediately stepped forward. The little ewe charged again, head down, and rammed into the dog as hard as she could. Unfortunately, she was so small that with such a short run up, although she halted the dog, she bounced off without doing any damage.

The dog laughed, tongue lolling. Acorn backed up, stamping threateningly, as the lamb huddled against her hind legs, too young to dream of running anywhere without her mother.

"Are you joking?" barked the dog. "You're so *tiny!* But not as tiny as *her.* Umm, I just want to get her in my mouth and *shake.* Go on, get out of my way..." The dog surged forward.

Acorn leaped to meet it, head down, but it barreled into her, carrying her to the ground in a frenzy of snapping teeth. Mandy heard a crack of breaking bone and smelled blood, as the ewe's squeal of agony cut through the cacophony of bleating.

"DROP HER!" Mandy used human words the dog should understand. "*Bad* dog. LET GO!"

Too intent on its victim, the dog didn't listen, but by that time Mandy was there. She swung the stick and brought it slamming into the dog, which was knocked off the mother sheep with a shocked yelp. But the dog leaped straight back up, attention still fixed on Acorn, who struggled to rise and protect her lamb, bleating terribly as her weight fell on her foreleg.

"LEAVE HER!" Mandy stepped in between as the dog sprang.

The dog stopped mid-lunge and stared at her over a long length of excitedly flailing tongue and a lot of very sharp teeth.

"What do you mean, leave her?" it barked. "I've never smelled anything so exciting in my life; never tasted anything so good! And the way they *run!* I've just gotta chase them!" Its head lowering, it tried to edge around Mandy, who moved sideways to stop it. "And I caught one," it panted, tail lashing from side to side in big, proud strokes. "I *caught* that one. It's mine! And the tiny one! Mine!"

"No, she's *not* yours! Aaand you're aaa *very* baaad dog. Good dogs don't chaaase sheep." She bleated that, since it was a rather more complicated idea to try to get across.

"Who are you to say what good dogs do?" growled the dog indignantly, attention on her now. "*You* smell good too..." It began to slink forward, menace in every pawfall. "Perhaps I'll catch *you*."

Her sheepy nature would've had her halfway across the field screaming at the top of her voice, but her human side took hold of her sheepy nature and sat on it. Those particular sheepy instincts would not save her friend and her little lamb.

She stamped her foot much as Acorn had done and tossed her head just as threateningly. Then, since her two-legged self had never actually been all that good at head butting things, she brandished the stick at the dog.

114

It made a satisfying swiping noise in the air just in front of the dog's nose. "If you come aaanywhere near me, I will *clout* you agaaain. Even haaarder!"

The dog realized—belatedly—that it was no longer in control of the situation. "But...but," it yapped plaintively, "you can't do that! You're just a big lamb. Wait..." It sniffed the air with increasing confusion. "A little girl? No...you're bleating—must be a lamb, but—wait...a...a... What *are* you?"

"I'm aaa haaalf-sheep girl, aaas it haaappens," bleated Mandy, acutely conscious of poor Acorn, who'd now collapsed in the grass, panting in pain, but knowing she needed to deal with the dog before anything else. "But aaas far aaas you're concerned I'm aaa girl, aaand you'll treat me aaas such! So *whaaat* do you do when I say, *'bad dog'*?" She *spoke* those two words in a very stern voice.

The dog had absolutely no desire to upset little girls. As a Labrador, one of its goals in life was to please as many little girls as it possibly could. Mandy's tone and human speech overruled any lingering concerns as to what she was. It dropped to its belly and whined for forgiveness.

"Do you know whaaat haaappens to dogs thaaat chaaase sheep in this vaaalley?"

The Labrador whined that it did not.

"They don't get aaany treats for aaa whole week aaand if they still chaaase sheep, they get shot!" Mandy

115

put the end of the stick to her shoulder like a shotgun and mimed firing at the dog.

The Labrador stared at her in horror. "No *treats?* For a whole *week?* That's...how long is that? That sounds... sounds like a very, very long time..."

"Quite. So you'd better not do this aaagain. Your maaaster will hear aaabout this aaas it is, aaand I'm sure one week without treats is enough to laaast you a lifetime."

The Labrador agreed, whimpering pitifully.

"Now, go straaaight home aaand don't go waaandering without your maaaster aaagain!"

The Labrador leaped up and streaked across the field. The sheep fled again as it came near.

"Ooh...sheep..." The dog veered slightly towards them.

"No treats!" threatened Mandy, shaking the stick.

The dog ran off home.

Mandy immediately crouched beside the young mother, who now lay shaking in pain. "Lie still," she bleated softly, "Lie still, Aaacorn."

"Maaandy? My laaamb, oh, my laaamb." Acorn made another frantic attempt to get up. "The house-wolf will eat my laaamb, Maaandy..."

"It's aaall right, Aaacorn," bleated Mandy. "It's okaaay, I drove the house-wolf aaaway. Leaf is saaafe."

Acorn had grown up at Mandy's house two years earlier, after Mr. Fletcher sent the tiny premature lamb down there in a last-ditch attempt to save her life. Fortunately, it had been the Easter holidays and Mandy had been able to give her new friend almost round-the-clock care, eventually nursing her to full health.

When the lambing season had ended this year, everyone assumed undersized Acorn wasn't going to have a lamb. Mr. Fletcher put her in with last year's lambs for the summer (she was still only about their size, for all Mandy's care), hoping she would have a lamb the following year. Everyone, from Mandy, to Mr. Fletcher, to Acorn herself, had been astonished when Mandy had popped in to see her friend one morning a few weeks ago, only to find her busily licking a teeny-weeny little lamb, perfectly formed for all its small size.

"Stop pushing her," Mandy told Leaf firmly, as she pressed up against her mother, seeking reassurance. "You'll hurt her leg." The lamb was too young to understand properly, so Mandy moved her around to Acorn's haunches, since it was her front leg that was broken.

Acorn bleated anxiously, wanting her lamb where she could see her.

"It's okaaay, Aaacorn, she's right there. She's saaafe. You protected her really well; you were so braaave. Now, don't worry about this leg of yours. I think you're going to be fine. I'll splint it aaand taaake you to Mr. Fletcher. He'll be aaable to taaake caaare of thaaat bite properly."

Mandy's fingers, with their hard, hoofy coating, put things like sewing that required fine motor control and good grip out of her reach. And that ragged bite was going to need stitches.

She headed to the nearest bush to find small branches for a makeshift splint.

"Maaandy, Maaandy, thaaank you!" Panting, the other sheep gathered around her. "You saaaved us, Maaandy."

"Oh, you're welcome," she bleated. As it happened, her legs felt suspiciously jelly-like. Facing down big house-wolves—that was, dogs—was not her idea of fun at all.

"Aaare you aaall okaaay?" She looked around as she hurried back to where Acorn lay shivering with her lamb huddled against her, still terrified by the never before experienced horror of the dog.

"We're fine, Maaandy, thaaanks to you," bleated the sheep. "Thaaat dog waaas so slow and clumsy!"

"Faaalling over its paaaws!"

"Couldn't decide who to chaaase!"

The sheep laughed nervously. She knew and they knew that the dog hadn't been slow and clumsy enough, but she joined them in making light of the situation.

"Silly dog," she bleated. "It'll be in trouble now! You won't need to worry aaabout it aaagain. No treats for aaa *week!* It'll be lucky if it gets aaany treats for aaa month, aaafter Mr. Fletcher's through with its maaaster, but it probably wouldn't haaave believed me, would it?"

"Silly dog," bleated the sheep. "Whaaat a silly dog, messing with Maaandy Laaamb!"

Mandy blushed and crouched beside Acorn again. "Mr. Fletcher will set this properly," she told her gently, though she knew Acorn wouldn't entirely understand what she meant. "I'm just going to do something to stop it from hurting too much whilst I caaarry you to the faaarm. But it might be aaa bit painful while I do it. Be braaave."

Acorn did her best while Mandy bound the bleeding leg with big dock leaves, but she still cried out as Mandy fastened the sticks in place with a couple of stretchy bracelets that she'd forgotten to remove before setting off for Mr. Fletcher's—how lucky that seemed, now!

Mr. Fletcher's... Bother, she should be there by now. Well, *this* was an unavoidable delay.

"Okaaay, let's get you to the faaarm." She hefted her friend up into her arms, eliciting another choked off bleat of pain. "Oh, I'm sorry, Aaacorn! Mr. Fletcher will haaave something to maaake it feel better."

She set off across the field as fast as she could. Leaf followed closely, beginning to panic again.

"I'm taaaking her to Mr. Fletcher," Mandy told her, though she really was too young to understand. "Mr.

119

Fletcher will sort your mummy's leg out. Everything will be fine." She knew she might have to say the last bit again and again until they reached the farmyard. Animals just didn't remember things the way people did. They'd remember things they knew, or events that had happened to them if something reminded them, but their minds just weren't...organized...the way humans' were.

She could feel poor Acorn's blood soaking into her fleece. Even undersized Acorn was almost more than an eleven-year-old could manage, even one part-sheep herself. All the same... Mandy picked up her hoofy feet and ran.

Get MANDY LAMB AND THE FULL MOON from your favorite retailer today!

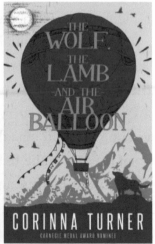

ABOUT THE AUTHOR

Corinna Turner has been writing since she was fourteen and likes strong protagonists with plenty of integrity. Although she spends as much time as possible writing, she cannot keep up with the flow of ideas, for which she offers thanks—and occasional grumbles!—to the Holy Spirit. She is the author of over twenty-five books, including the Carnegie Medal Nominated I Am Margaret series, and her work has been translated into four languages. She was awarded the St. Katherine Drexel award in 2022.

She is a Lay Dominican with an MA in English from Oxford University and lives in the UK. She is a member of a number of organizations, including the Society of Authors, Catholic Teen Books, Catholic Reads, the Angelic Warfare Confraternity, and the Sodality of the Blessed Sacrament. She used to have a Giant African Land Snail, Peter, with a 6½" long shell, but now makes do with a cactus and a campervan.

Get in touch with Corinna...

Facebook: Corinna Turner

Twitter: @CorinnaTAuthor

Don't forget to sign up for

NEWS
&
FREE SHORT STORIES
at:

www.UnSeenBooks.com

All Free/Exclusive content subject to availability.

Made in United States
Troutdale, OR
02/21/2024

17856769R10083